Growing Up White

In the Heart of Memphis

David May

Growing Up White
In the Heart of Memphis

Indented, italicized paragraphs are of incidents in the civil rights movement. Most of them are taken from the "Timeline of the African-American Civil Rights Movement (1954–68) from Wikipedia, the free encyclopedia." They are presented so that you can see what was going on in the world around me as I grew up.

ISBN-13: 978-1979198776

ISBN-10: 1979198772

CONTENTS

INTRODUCTION

What does it mean to have grown up White in the 1940s and 1950s in the heart of Memphis, Tennessee? Do I owe someone an apology? Or does history owe me an apology?

Sitting here seventy-six years later, I have one son who marches with Black Lives Matter. Matt doesn't like for people to counter the BLM slogan with "all lives matter" because that misses the point. The point is that it is Black people who are being shot down from sea to shining sea. Matt has a great heart. He loves everyone and he has a special love for people who have been disadvantaged, regardless of the cause of their disadvantage. He reminds me of a man who lived in war torn Israel a couple of millennia ago.

I have another son who, fairly late in life, fulfilled his lifelong dream of becoming a Police Officer. After gaining his Master's degree in Social Work and spending several years working in Child Protection, Mark became a Saint Paul Police Department beat cop. He loves the job still, but I think he was blindsided by the hate he sometimes encounters because of the uniform. His dream was to be the well-loved neighborhood police officer who settled disagreements and generally made life better for everyone. Like Matt, Mark holds no animosity toward anyone. But he was intentionally hit one day during a march by a piece of concrete thrown off an overpass. He is frankly frightened by all the guns on the streets and the propensity to point them at police officers.

Mark and Matt love each other, though they don't necessarily see all the issues alike these days.

My wife, Charlene, and I also have a Black son, Ricky; a Black son-in-law, Cordell; and a beautiful bi-racial grandson, Phoenix. More on them later.

A friend expressed concern that this book will imply that because she is White she is racist. That is not my intention at all. I don't do that. One of my pet peeves is folk who, in their thinking, put people into large groups and make assumptions about the whole group. Stereotyping people like that robs them of their individuality and ultimately of their free will. We are all given the ability to make up our own minds and to change them whenever we want. None of us is required to think like other people think.

A note about capitalizing "Black" and "White": I did research on whether to capitalize the words "Black" or "White" or both. There is an excellent article on the subject in the "Columbia Journalism Review" by Merrill Perlman, found here: https://www.cjr.org/analysis/language_corner_1.php

The conclusion seemed to be that it is "fielders' choice." So, in the interest of fairness and respect, I have chosen to capitalize both words throughout this book.

A word about my writing style: I am not a novelist. I don't notice much detail. I can't tell you the color of the shirt of the man I had breakfast with this morning, let alone 40 years ago. I don't remember what the temperature was or which way the wind was blowing. This is just the basic story: what happened and who said what. I hope it is helpful, nevertheless, and maybe a quicker read without all the detail.

The impetus for this effort has been my desire to contribute to the conversation about race in America in the early 21st century, and particularly about the relationship between Black churches and White churches. The church should be leading the way toward reconciliation of the races and as long as 10:00 A.M. Sunday morning is the most segregated hour of the week, we are lying down on the job. That is a much more complicated issue than it first appears. More on that later.

This is not my autobiography. The few elaborations on our children are just to add to the intention of the book. I have met a lot of interesting people and have been on many adventures that are not included here. And I have omitted loads of funny stories because they do not contribute to my purpose.

It has been difficult choosing which stories to tell. If I tell too much, it becomes just me talking about me. If I tell too little, you lose the context for the really important parts.

As you read, look for three threads. First, I have tried to listen for God and follow His lead. But, second, I have always had a strong tendency to go along to get along and that has detracted me from doing the right thing. I have had a lot of opportunities to "hold up a light in the darkness," but have opted to keep it under cover. And, third, I believe I am in the process of discovering a road toward doing the right thing. Please pray for me as you read.

As you read my story, you may find it hard to believe that I was so gullible, so naïve. I do. But this story, to the best of my ability, tells it the way it happened. That may be part of what makes the story useful today. This is the story of the enlightenment of one young man who lived through the Civil Rights Movement, who sympathized with it, cheered for it even, loved the music of it, but who didn't do anything significant about it. I believe my experiences were rather typical.

This story is not presented as an answer for all of us, but it may lead some of us to an answer. Maybe it is an apology. Maybe it is a penance. Maybe it is a call to action. Or maybe it is just a story. But it is my story. I hope you will appreciate it.

PROLOUGE

Whose U.S. Is This Anyway? A brief timeline of ethnicity in the land now known as the United States

The part of North America that we claim as our country was once the property of a number of bands of native peoples. They roamed freely in established territories, trying to stay out of each other's way or trying to take part of another group's land. Some scientists believe they were immigrants like the rest of us, but they were the first immigrants.

Then came a long series of refugee groups from Europe. They went to war with the native people and eventually conquered them. In 1776 the Europeans declared that they were independent of Europe. They subsequently established a formal government and put it in charge of the land. Then they set out deliberately to remove the native people from the land to make room for the Europeans to take ownership, including passing the Indian Removal Act, signed by President Andrew Jackson in 1830.

The new "Americans" of European descent bought Africans who had been enslaved in their home countries and had them work, unwillingly, on their farms and in their houses. Though the government was democratic in nature, neither the African slaves nor the European-descended women were allowed to vote. The country was run by White men.

While the White Americans were moving west, expanding the borders of their country by defeating the native people, Hispanic people from the south were also moving their borders north into the same territory. Wars ensued between the former Europeans and the Hispanic peoples. The Europeans won and firm lines were drawn with the Europeans on one side and the Hispanics on the other. Today, the Americans of European descent are trying to build a wall along those lines to keep the Hispanics and others out. As time went on, people began to immigrate from all over the world, adding Asian people and more Europeans to the mix – not so much Africans.

At the present time many Americans of European descent are feeling threatened by the growing numbers of people of African, Asian and Hispanic descent. Many are especially afraid and even angry at the fact that Americans are buying all kinds of goods from other countries, but my response has always been "Little Chinese children have to eat, too."

Black people, whose ancestors were brought here as slaves, are still being mistreated, in spite of a successful Civil Rights Movement which won them many legal rights.

I am a U.S. Marine Corps veteran and I love this country. One of my favorite songs is Lee Greenwood's "Proud to be an American." Though I likely would have written it "Pleased to be an American." I think being proud is about something in which I had a choice. But I can't pretend that her history has been fair and honest, especially in her dealings with people who are not White.

An underlying theme in this book is the notion of White privilege. While I don't point it out directly in each instance, you will see how it played out to my advantage time after time in the story.

I am White, of European descent. I grew up in a part of the country inhabited by large numbers of descendants of slaves. This is my story.

CHAPTER 1

THE UNION AVENUE CHURCH – PART 1

I was born in Memphis on November 13, 1941 – less than a month before the Japanese bombed the U.S. Navy, docked at Pearl Harbor, Hawaii, bringing the United States into what became known as the Second World War (WW2). Emmett Till was born four months earlier on the South side of Chicago. More about that later.

At the time I didn't know anything about war, or about Civil Rights, or about Charlene, the baby girl I would meet seventeen months later who would eventually become the love of my life.

I don't remember hating Japanese people. By the 1950s, ten years after Pearl Harbor, our church was supporting missionaries in Japan, so I think that represents the attitude of my mentors and peers toward the Japanese.

A little over 20 years later, I was stationed in Okinawa where I lived and worked among Japanese people. The role of their ancestors in WW2 never occurred to me. Some would call me naïve, but I don't hold you accountable for any evil your forefathers may have committed, nor do I give you credit for any good they may have accomplished. We each must answer for our own actions.

When I think of the Japanese, I often think of Mr. Myiagi, the hero from "The Karate Kid." I think of the era before Silicon Valley, when everything cool and new and technical came out of Japan. And I also think of the Japanese built van we drive, with over 230,000 miles on it and counting. I didn't hear about the internment camps until years after the war was over. Do I have an excuse for my ignorance? I am not sure I need one; it was the nature of the time in which I lived.

The Union Avenue Church of Christ played a major role for Charlene and me as we grew up. It had been the first Church of Christ in Memphis and had grown to 1000 members by the time we came along. We were taught to love God and the importance of obeying Him. A favorite memory and a tribute to the Union Avenue church is of me standing at the end of my crib, kicking out the rhythm and singing at the top of my lungs, "Up from the grave He arose!"

That scene, of the grave and of the angel standing there alone, is still very important to me. I have often said that the four most important words in the Bible are the ones spoken by that angel to those who were looking for the Lord: "He is not here." Jesus got up and walked out of the grave on a Sunday morning, proving once and for all that we have nothing to be afraid of in this life or in the next one.

I remember discovering God's grace at the Call Street church in Tallahassee, Florida, several years after we were married. I was amazed to learn how forgiving God is. So, I am thinking that there wasn't so much said about that at Union Avenue in the '40s and '50s. The first year we were married we also discovered that some ministers had bizarre, detailed ideas about what obedience to God entailed, so it appears that Union was not of that ilk either, but more of a "middle of the road" church with more emphasis on obedience and evangelism than on what God has done and is doing for us.

Union Avenue was, of course, all White, but I do remember occasions when numbers of Black people would attend. It was always when we had a special speaker – maybe a missionary giving a report or a well-known preacher from another state. The Black people would all sit in the balcony. I never met any of them. That was probably intentional on somebody's part. I suppose an invitation had been given to one or more of the Black churches in town.

I never saw a Black person standing at the pulpit and never heard a Black person speak in the Union Avenue Building. I never knew anyone from any of the Black churches and our congregation never had singings, pot luck meals or other acts of worship with them. It seems to me now that I should have noticed that and asked questions about it, but none of the other teens noticed either. It was never a topic of conversation. Looking back on the situation makes me sad. It seems I was part of some great conspiracy that I was totally unaware of.

I do remember that there was a prominent Black preacher, Brother Marshall Keeble, from Nashville. He was spoken of with respect, as was the preacher from the local Black church. I never met either of them, though Charlene heard Brother Keeble speak several times in northern Mississippi. Back then, all adult church members were referred to as "Brother" or "Sister" regardless of race. Looking back at it, I think that must have been different from the societal norm which would have called all Black people by their first name.

We lived in a protected environment. I never heard Black people put down or demeaned by the adults I grew up around. On the other hand, I never heard any expression of regret for their circumstance. They just were not a topic of conversation – like non-entities.

The Youth Group

By the time we were teens in the 1950's, I don't think youth ministers were yet acceptable among the churches of Christ, but Union Avenue saw a need. They hired a full-time song leader. Today he would be called a worship leader. Bob Riggs, though, spent most of his time with us kids. We were formed into a chorus. Churches of Christ did not and do not typically have a church choir that sings in the worship service. We are almost all a capella churches, meaning we sing without instrumental accompaniment and therefore do a good bit of training in singing.

Our group learned all the funeral and wedding songs and were constantly performing at such events. We also learned many hymns including some of the more complicated ones with four-part harmony and gave performances for the church at times other than the regular worship times. We went to great lengths to uphold the principles of the Restoration Movement from which we had evolved. That included such adages as, "Speak where the Bible speaks and be silent where the Bible is silent." The second part of that is the hardest.

The youth chorus was our youth group. We bowled, played miniature golf, and went to movies together. We were frequently joined by the youth from other (White) churches in town. We never saw or had any word from the Black churches. It was as if they did not exist. Kind of scary.

All our friends were in the chorus. At Christmas time, we walked miles of corridors at the local veterans' hospital singing Christmas carols and we put on Christmas concerts. We were truly a White Christmas. We had no idea what our Black brothers and sisters were doing and gave no thought to it. Somehow, I think it should at least have occurred to me. Maybe I could have done something.

CHAPTER 2

The Wonder Years

My dad was drafted into the Army for WW2 and was assigned to the Army Air Corps, the predecessor to the U.S. Air Force. His whole tour was spent in south Texas, reconditioning bomber engines. Emmet Till's dad was killed in Germany.

My childhood in Memphis was ideal. I remember playing games in the street in front of our house on Vinton Avenue. There were Louie and Jimmy and a slightly younger boy named "Baby Chick." If he had any other name, I never heard it. There was also a girl or two. We played "Mother May I?", "Kick the Can" and some other games I don't remember.

I especially remember the thunderstorms. I loved walking barefoot in the warm water in the gutters and racing sticks we dubbed "sail boats". We were of course all White – never gave any thought to the Black kids, probably playing in the gutters not so very far away.

In the late '40s and early '50s when I would have been about eight to twelve years old, I had this fantasy. I never told anyone about it until a few months ago. I imagined I had been designated to become something like Supreme Benevolent Ruler of the Universe. And invisible beings of some kind were watching after me, guiding and protecting me. Today I am thinking that was God's way of letting me know everything was going to be okay, though I probably added the part about Supreme Ruler. I have decided that the invisible beings were angels.

CHAPTER 3

Mama Ran Away

My mother left home when I was eight. The only children were my big brother, Cecil, and me. He is nine-and-a-half years older than me and mother's timing was such that she left just as he finished high school and went off to college. I have wondered about that. Was she waiting for him to finish high school? Don't know.

Mother moved in with a chain-smoking, heavy beer-drinking clerk from the local Weona grocery store. There were no chain groceries back then and the Weona chain was new. The name is pronounced as if it were "We own a" grocery store. Each store was locally owned and the groceries were provided by the parent company. Dony didn't own it. He was the clerk.

Mother's departure was devastating for me. It marked my transition to adolescence. I was not supposed to know what was coming, but I picked up on a lot of not so subtle clues like mother coming in the front door just in time to make my breakfast before time for me to go to school. And her collapsing in tears after she took a call from one of the elders at church.

Once the divorce was final, my mother wanted me to go to her wedding in West Memphis, across the Mississippi River in Arkansas. They didn't tell me where they wanted me to go, just that they wanted me to go with them. But I had figured it out. I declined. I wasn't formally informed until I met my mother for lunch one day and she showed me her new diamond ring. Interestingly, my mother never said anything negative about my daddy. He was a good man and she knew it. Her departure is still a puzzle to me.

That year was hard on me as a third grader. In my senior year in college I took a Freshman Creative Writing course. I had tested out of that course at Harding University where I went my first year, but at the University of Mississippi (Ole Miss), my alma mater, they wanted me to take it. I wrote an essay about the year my mother left and my feelings about it. It was still on my mind. In fact, I still have a copy of that essay.

But my mother deserves more than the story of her moving out. She had always wanted a little pink house and they saved and bought one.

Mother was a caretaker. She went by her mother's house every morning and every evening going to and from work to take care of her ailing and ageing father, who I knew as "Will". My Daddy called him "Mr. Will".

After Will died, Mother eventually took her mother into her little pink house and cared for her until she died. Then there was a cousin of some kind that she took in and nursed until he died. He was followed by Dony who needed a caretaker until he died.

As I was returning Mother to her little pink house from Dony's funeral, her knee gave way on the steps from the driveway to the kitchen. It was the first indication of a disease that gradually hardened all her muscles. Eventually, she had to be in a nursing home. She even lost her ability to speak, though her mind was always sharp. The staff at the home sometimes mistook her muteness for lack of mental ability.

We lived in Florida at the time and she was in Kosciusco, Mississippi, where my brother was the

President of Magnolia Bible college. We got there once or twice a year, but mother never complained. She always had a big smile for us when we arrived and again when we left.

There is one more thing I want you to know, though, about my mother. Her neighborhood was gradually inhabited by Black families. For many blocks in each direction, she was the only White person.

I never heard a negative comment from her about it. She made friends with her new neighbors and lived happily in her little pink house until her health forced her move to the nursing home in Kosciusco. I am proud of her difference from the Union Avenue Church.

Nina

I called my mother's mother Nina, pronounced "Nen-nah". When Mother left home, Nina stepped up to fill the gap.

Nina rode two city busses across town to be there when I got home from school. Many times through the years, I heard my daddy express his deeply-held appreciation for Nina's sacrificial love and concern for me.

I soon started to rely on my bicycle for transportation. It was a mile and a half from home to my daddy's barbershop, three and a half to Nina's apartment and four and a half to the public housing unit she moved into shortly after. I lived on the bicycle, at the barbershop and at Nina's. Lots of afternoons I would go to the shop to read the comic books my dad kept there.

Nina was a non-attending member of the local Methodist church, but she did send in a contribution and get a bulletin in the mail. Her greatest love was for her two youngest grandchildren: my cousin, Sam, and me. Sam and I spent many a day at her apartment playing pretend games. When we were pre-school age, she took us downtown to have our pictures taken professionally – something none of us could afford, her included.

Nina had large pictures of John F. Kennedy and Franklin Delano Roosevelt on her walls, indicating, I think, her love for disadvantaged people and for those who operated to rescue them. She also had a large brass medallion with a picture of Roosevelt on it. It rests in sight on my dresser today.

As a young boy, I remember noticing that the Black mail carrier for the all-White housing project would stop at Nina's apartment for a glass of cold water. He would come in and sit at the kitchen table to drink it.

And then there was Forrest Park. Nina and I would often meet in Forrest Park, next to Gadsden Hospital, the city hospital that treated people without insurance. The park was between my house and hers and she would bring lunch for the two of us. It was a pleasant place with trees and people moving quietly about. I have fond memories of those times with my grandmother. I never thought to inquire about the name of the place or the man on the horse.

In the middle of the park was big statue of a guy on a horse – General Nathan Bedford Forrest. I didn't know it at the time, but Forrest was a Confederate General in the Civil War. He was a brilliant tactician, using guerrilla warfare when everyone else was trying to take land. Before the war, he had become one of the wealthiest men in Tennessee by trading slaves. After the war, Forrest became the first Grand Wizard of the Ku Klux Klan. I was amazed when doing research for this book and found that, though the name of the park has changed, the statute is still there. There are protests going on as I write and it may not be there much longer.

James

There was a Black man in my daddy's barbershop who shined shoes. The only name I ever heard for him was James. He had a stand in the corner where someone could climb up onto the chair to have his shoes shined. The customer would pay my dad for the shine when he paid for his haircut and Daddy would settle up with James at the end of every day. I never knew the financial details. James was a middle-aged man, but he was referred to as the shoe shine boy. I didn't pick up on the indignity of all that until later.

Ethel, Mavis and Callie Mae

Before she married my daddy, Charlene's mom, as poor as she was, employed a Black woman in her home. There were three in all, one at a time. Charlene and her siblings considered them as family and still speak fondly of these women.

"Latchkey Kid"

Daddy closed the shop at 6:00 p.m. and would cut the hair of anybody that got in the door by then. That put him leaving there between 6:30 and 7:00 most days - eleven hours after he opened the shop at 8:00 a.m. He was there five and a half days a week, closing at noon on Wednesday and all-day Sunday. Those were 55-60-hour weeks. I was pretty much on my own.

Most days we would meet for dinner at the Rainbow Café, halfway between the barbershop and home. After dinner, I would put my bike in the back seat of the car for a ride home. Eventually there was a server at the Rainbow who took a special liking to daddy, but that never went anywhere.

In the summertime, I went to scout camp for a week and to church camp for two weeks. The rest of the summer, I would stay with my grandparents, "Mom and Pop", on their farm in northeast Tennessee. It was about 100 miles from home, near the little town of Mason Hall. Most of my cousins lived close to them. Some of them actually lived in the little town. I remember that many days I would walk the three miles into Mason Hall to get a six-ounce coke, drink it, then walk back. It was a fun time. Later my Daddy bought me a horse and I rode him into town.

I won't say it was one of my favorite memories of that time, because it was hard work, but it is a memory I am glad I have. I picked cotton a couple of times. Even in that experience, I didn't see any Black people. I suppose the economics of the time prevented our family and friends from hiring anybody. I don't think they paid us kids anything.

The Mason Hall schools started early in the fall, then took a break for cotton picking. All the kids would go to the fields.

At Wildwood church camp I fell in love. I must have been about ten years old. Her name was Joan and she was from San Antonio. We tried writing after camp was over, but that only lasted a few weeks. Never knew what happened to her. A beautiful, little, black-haired girl.

One year my dad took my scout troop to Camp Kia Kima, the scout camp. It was over in Arkansas. He was not connected to the troop in any formal way, but they must have needed someone to take us, so he did. He was amazed (and, I think, proud) that I passed the swim test on the first try. The test was a requirement in order to go in the deeper part of the swimming area. His surprise was in spite of the fact that he had taught me to swim at the all-White city pool in Memphis.

CHAPTER 4

Newspaper Delivery

Stalin died March 5, 1953 at 74. I was 11. Nina was still coming to the house every afternoon. For several years after that she bragged on me for coming in the front door after delivering my newspapers that afternoon, holding up the paper with the banner headline and telling her Stalin was dead. I am guessing it was the very large print, bold headline that let me know it was important. I am still not sure what I did that was special, but I suspect Nina just thought anything I did was special. Every kid needs a cheerleader like I had in Nina.

My teen years were great. I was a free spirit. At about 12 I was considered old enough that Nina didn't have to make that cross-town trip every afternoon.

Before I was old enough to have my own newspaper delivery route, my brother, Cecil, sub-contracted the commercial part of his route to me. I delivered the paper to a couple of corner drug stores, a barbershop, one apartment building and the neighborhood movie theater. Though they were all White, there were no "Whites Only" signs anywhere. Everyone just knew the rules.

It was on my second paper route, in a more residential neighborhood, that I had my second encounter with bullies. The fellow who had the route before I did, came around one afternoon and took a newspaper I had left on somebody's porch and put in on the sidewalk out front. He had a buddy with him.

I didn't even know the guy, so I don't think he had anything against me personally. I guessed that he may not have given up the route willingly. I picked up the paper and went after him. I shoved the paper in his direction and told him to put it back where it belonged. He slapped me with his open hand and turned and walked away. I put the paper back, but I never saw or heard from him again.

I had very mixed emotions about that incident – a combination of embarrassment and anger. I was hurt by it.

Paperboys (they were all boys back then, but that's a different book) were independent contractors. We paid for the papers and collected from our customers, so we had some flexibility. We were all White. It never occurred to me to wonder who delivered the papers in the Black neighborhoods.

The Movies

Someone before me had worked out an arrangement with the Memphian movie theater wherein I gave them the paper for free and they let me in on Saturday afternoon without charge. Saturday afternoon was clearly kids' time at the movies: two full length movies, many of them westerns, most of them with John Wayne; a "short subject," frequently with Abbott and Costello; one or more cartoons and a newsreel.

It was about a break-even deal for both of us, but it boosted my ego considerably, being able to bypass the line of kids at the ticket booth and wave at the ticket taker as I went in.

One of the movies we saw was "Song of the South" with Uncle Remus (a slave), Brer Rabbit, Brer Fox, Brer Bear and a White boy. It was later excluded from video rental stores, libraries and other such places because of the depiction of Uncle Remus and his relationship with his owners. I loved the story and still do. The little boy loved Uncle Remus and his stories. His White parents tried to keep the two of them apart. I am not sure why it was taken off the shelves. It was an important movie in my mind.

New Orleans

With the help of some friends, I won a bus trip to New Orleans for signing up new newspaper customers. I was 14. The deadline date had arrived and I was still a few subscriptions short of the goal, but some of my friends wanted me to go with them to New Orleans. They went with me door to door in the apartment buildings. We got all but one signed up and were talking with this very reluctant young woman. She was persistently saying “No.” Time was almost up, so I offered the paper for free, if she would just sign the form. She did and I made the trip.

We stayed in the Roosevelt Hotel and roamed the French Quarter, sampling some of the local food. On the bus, I napped in the overhead luggage racks. On the way home one of the guys was passing around a deck of playing cards he had bought there with nudes on the back. I am not sure, but I believe even the nudes were all White. It was a pretty White world I lived in.

CHAPTER 5

American History – Southern Style

In 1953 I started Junior High in a local Christian School. I was in seventh grade. It was a pretty miserable year. I was a skinny, non-athletic kid and a small group of older boys bullied me all year long. This was my first encounter with bullies. Basically, I tried to stay away from them and hung out with a couple of other "unpopular" kids. Don't get me wrong, I had friends, but they tended not to be on the inside with the athletes and their hangers-on. It is still interesting to me that this was in a Christian school. I never encountered anything like it during my other 11 years in public schools.

But on top of that, the eighth-grade teacher doubled as the Bible teacher for the seventh grade and he clearly didn't like me. I don't remember any specifics now, but I was sure I did not want him to be my primary teacher the following year. Thinking about it now, his attitude toward me might have played into the eighth graders harassing me.

I talked with my dad about it and he allowed me to transfer to public school. When I wasn't supposed to be listening, I overheard Daddy's sisters giving him a hard time for letting me switch schools. He expressed his confidence in me, a twelve-year-old, and in my judgment. I had a great supporter in my dad.

Years later, the eighth-grade teacher who didn't like me confessed to Cecil 3, my nephew, that he and my brother had applied for the same preaching job and my brother got the job. He told C3 that he had been mean to me all year long. So, don't be too quick to dismiss the observations of your young people.

Ms. Fesmire

The following year, I was in the eighth grade in the public Junior High near our home. Ms. Fesmire, my American History teacher, became my favorite teacher of all time. She was a masterful storyteller and was the inspiration for me taking a story-telling class from the Guthrie Theater in Minneapolis years later. She was also my Civics teacher in the ninth grade and is at least partly responsible for my lifelong interest in politics.

After the ninth-grade, Ms. Fesmire asked me to accompany her on her annual road trip to south Florida to visit her nephew. I accepted; then told my dad. I remember being surprised that he had any reluctance to let me go. It took me awhile to figure out that he didn't know my favorite teacher, or why she would ask me to go along on such a journey. He did relent and I went along. I don't know whether he ever spoke with her about it.

Looking back on it, most of our American History class was about the Civil War with a little before and a little after. Less than ninety years after the war, in Memphis, Ms. Fesmire taught her all-White class from a Southern point of view.

Remember that she taught Civics as well. She taught the Civil War as a war over states' rights. In her mind, it was a war about how much liberty did the states have vs how much authority did the federal government have.

Not much was said about slavery. It was probably implied, but it was not the stated issue in our class. Even after our road trip I still don't know what Ms. Fesmire thought about slavery or about Black people.

Though it was something I might could have deduced from her silence, it wasn't something we talked about. It never occurred to me that Ms. Fesmire might have been a racist. I hope not. She was otherwise a very kind and gentle woman.

> *May 17, 1954 – In Brown v. Board of Education of Topeka, Kansas, the U.S. Supreme Court ruled against the "separate but equal" doctrine, making segregated public schools illegal.*
>
> *September 16, 1954 – Mississippi abolished all public schools with an amendment to its State Constitution. Private segregation academies are founded for white students.*

1954 was the year we finished American History in the spring and started Civics in the fall. I don't remember discussion of either of these events. It is kind of chilling – as if Black people didn't exist and the Civil Rights Movement didn't happen.

CHAPTER 6

Emmett Till

On August 25, 1955, Emmett Till was murdered in Money, Mississippi, about two hours south of Memphis. In the aftermath of that event I began to learn about the extent, if not the effects, of racism. In fact, at that time I began to realize the existence of Black people and something of their status.

Having just turned 14, Emmett was four months older than I was. I was still 13 and would be until November. Emmett was visiting relatives in Mississippi from his home in Chicago. He was not familiar with the cultural norms enforced on Black people in the south and made the fatal mistake of flirting with a White woman. The woman, years later, admitted embellishing the story when she told it to her husband

and to others, including the jury that tried the two men who brutally murdered Emmett.

Two White men, one of them the woman's husband, kidnapped and beat Emmett and shot him in the head. They used barbed wire to tie his body to a 74-pound fan from a cotton gin and threw it into the Tallahatchie River.

Despite credible witnesses and confessions by both men, they were acquitted by a White jury. For more on the story check out "Getting Away with Murder: The True Story of the Emmett Till Case" by Chris Crowe.

Emmett's mother had his unrecognizable body carried back to Chicago and decided to hold an open casket funeral. That decision has been credited with kicking off the Civil Rights Movement. Rosa Parks has also been credited with being the catalyst that started the movement when she started the Montgomery bus boycott four months later by sitting down in the White section of a city bus, but she has been quoted as saying that she was thinking about Emmett at the time.

Photographs of Emmett's mangled body were run in a local Chicago newspaper and Jet Magazine. Look Magazine in January published the written confessions of the two men. People all over the world could see the results of local "justice" that summer in Mississippi.

I never saw the photograph until I was doing the research for this book, but somewhere along the road I heard the story. Perhaps I read about it In the Memphis Commercial Appeal, the morning newspaper that I had graduated to delivering by that time. Somehow the fact that Emmett was about my age had a profound effect on me. I never thought of doing anything about it. In fact, I don't think I ever even talked about it with anyone. As a loner, it was not in my nature to discuss whatever was going on in my head.

To illustrate that point, I had learned at Union Avenue about the "age of accountability." That was the age at which a girl or boy became aware of sin, knew he or she was a sinner and had better do something about it. It was generally thought that 12 was the magic age, and in a group of 1000 people there was a regular procession of 12-year-olds being baptized. But as I was approaching my eleventh birthday I became increasingly aware of my spiritual condition and ever more aware of the possibility of the car-wreck-on-the-way-home-from-church that the preachers talked about from time to time.

One Sunday morning I could wait no longer. I knew I was supposed to wait until I was 12, but I also knew that I might not live that long. So, at the end of the sermon when the preacher gave the invitation, I jumped up out of my pew and made my way to the front, asking to be baptized. To their credit, nothing was said about my age and I was buried in the water and forgiven for my sins.

Now you may ask what kind of sin resume could a ten-year-old have accrued, but I knew mine was egregious. The point here is that I didn't talk to anyone about it. First, I was not about to list my sins for anyone. That was between me and God and it was none of anyone else's business. And second, as an independent child, I knew what my thinking was, that I was not about to be swayed by anyone, and therefore I did not need or want to talk to anyone.

One could say that I kept my own counsel. And that is what I did with my knowledge of Emmet Till's murder and the acquittal of his confessed murderers. Thinking all the time, "That could have been me."

December 1, 1955 – Rosa Parks refused to give up her seat on a bus, starting the Montgomery Bus Boycott.

CHAPTER 7

"Eww, take that out of your mouth"

The same year Emmett was killed I became aware of the attitude of some of my White compatriots toward Black people. It was my first year at Memphis Central, a three-year high school. With our school ID we rode the city busses to school. I still think that is a nifty idea. Minneapolis does this. The students become more a part of the community and it avoids the purchase and operation of a lot of school busses.

I would occasionally go back to the front row of Black people and sit beside someone there. So, I must have had some inkling that Black people were looked down on, but I had no idea of the strength of those feelings in some Whites, especially in my peers.

I had joined ROTC. I think all boys were required to join the first year. It was optional in the Junior and Senior years. No telling what the girls were doing – probably sewing, cooking, washing dishes and the like.

ROTC is the Reserve Officer Training Corps. It is military training. Actually, the high school version is JROTC, the "J" standing for "Junior". The real ROTC is a college program, but we still called it ROTC in High School.

There was this really cool boy who was in some kind of leadership position in ROTC. He was good-looking and very popular. I admired him and had picked him out as a role model. One day at lunch he happened to be right in front of me in line. I was trying to juggle my books and the food I was putting on my tray, keep moving the tray along the line and have my money ready for my milk. Money for milk was a single coin. I am thinking it was a nickel back then. In order to manage everything, it was my custom to hold the nickel between my teeth.

RCB (Really Cool Boy) saw me and got a horrible, ugly expression on his face and said "Eww, take that out of your mouth; some n***** may have had that in his mouth." I can still see that disgusted expression, though I have long forgotten the boy's name. My hero image of the boy fell in crumbles at my feet.

Until that time I had no idea that some White people had ideas like that about Black people. I was horrified. I felt dirty for knowing the boy and for having respected him. I will admit that putting a nickel in your mouth is probably not a good idea (though I still might do it given the right circumstances), but the race of someone who might have touched the coin before had no bearing on the question, neither then nor now.

And I am sure that another factor in my view of the situation was his giving me an order. I was a free spirit and he had ordered me to remove the nickel. He did not offer me information or a point of view, he gave me an order. That did not sit well with me.

That incident, along with Emmett's murder, was the awakening of my awareness to serious racial tensions. Call me naïve, but I was blind to the strength of feeling with which Black people were looked down upon by the White populace.

"Hebrew High" and the Mauzy Sisters

Central High was the oldest school in town. It was a college prep school and there was another school, "Tech High", nearby. Central gave out letters to its sports players like all the others, except that Central didn't give out Cs, it gave out Hs. That was a part of a long tradition. They started giving out Hs, standing for "High School," when they were the only one in town. The tradition continues even today. In the 50s the H on the letter jackets, combined with the fact that most of the Jewish kids in town chose Central, led to it being known informally as "Hebrew High."

And that story leads me to the Mauzy sisters (pronounced Mo-zee). In the 1950s, at least in my part of the world, female teachers were almost all "spinsters". Today's Dictionary.com says the word is disparaging and offensive, but I don't believe it was so much so back then. Sometimes it was hyphenated into "spinster-ladies". It simply meant that they were unmarried beyond the usual age for marrying.

I only remember three of my high school teachers. There was the French teacher whom I remember primarily because of the derogatory name the students had for her, and then, there were the Mauzy sisters. We assumed they were twins, but they were probably just sisters. They were short, older Jewish ladies. Both were very much in charge of their classrooms. Their names were Grace and Laura. Grace taught English, Laura math. My time in their classrooms was delightful.

Grace taught literature. We read Beowulf and Chaucer and Shakespeare and all the later great writers. She made them come to life. A few years later, though, at Ole Miss I had a mandatory sophomore literature course using the exact same book. We were supposed to read it on our own and take tests. I was convinced that I didn't need to read it again, because I had already read it, albeit four years prior. I finally passed the course, on the third try, without re-reading the book. Didn't help my grade point average any though. I loved Grace Mauzy.

Laura taught Algebra and Geometry. I especially liked the geometry class. Unlike other math teachers, she didn't have us memorize the formulas and proofs; she had us figure them out. That has served me well through the years. I have often said that Laura taught us how to think and Grace taught us what to think about.

On the web pages dedicated to certain graduating years right after I left there, student after student told Grace and Laura stories.

Grace retired very shortly after I graduated and died while I was in college. At the funeral, one of Grace's students told Laura that Grace was the best teacher he had ever had. Laura's response: "That was because you never had me for math."

Charlene

In my junior year of high school, my dad married Charlene's mother. About that time, I was dating several girls, but I never "dated" Charlene. We had always been good friends. After our parents married, we occasionally went to a movie together and almost always showed up together, along with her older sister, Maxine, at youth group outings. I liked the arrangement, but I think Charlene was frustrated by it.

CHAPTER 8

Little Rock Central High

Little Rock Central High School was something of a sister school to Memphis Central. It held the same status in Little Rock that Memphis Central did in Memphis.

We even played football against them. My first year at Memphis Central I rode a chartered bus taking Memphis students to the game in Little Rock. Today it is 137 miles and a two-hour drive. It would have been longer then, before the interstates were built. The game was a 7-7 tie, and I left there with some affinity for Little Rock Central. It was, at that time, also an all-White school.

My ears perked up the next year on September 4, 1957, when nine Black students were refused admission there. I was 15, starting my junior year.

"The Little Rock Nine", as they came to be called, had been hand-picked and recruited by Daisy Bates, the president of the Arkansas chapter of the National Association for the Advancement of Colored People (NAACP).

The Supreme Court decision, Brown vs Board of Education, May 17, 1954, had declared that segregation in schools was unconstitutional, but many of the southern states were resisting. Governor Orval Faubus was using the Arkansas National Guard to keep the nine students out.

I am not sure where President Eisenhower's heart was, but he knew where the nation was on the issue, so he countered with the famous 101st Airborne Division of the U.S. Army, famous for parachuting into France in the dark morning hours of June 6, 1944 – "D-Day" for World War 2. The nine new students at Little Rock Central were escorted into the building and were guarded for the entire school year by the nation's finest. Ernest Green became the first black student to graduate from there.

I followed the story closely, not knowing that I would encounter the 101st Airborne again in a similar situation five years later.

September 2, 1958 – Governor J. Lindsay Almond, Jr. of Virginia threatens to shut down any school if it is forced to integrate. September 18 – Governor Lindsay closes two schools in Charlottesville, Virginia, and six in Norfolk on Sep. 27.

Memphis Schools

Memphis schools were integrated in a different manner. In 1961, 13 Black first graders entered four Memphis elementary schools.

> *"When these students desegregated Memphis City Schools there was no violence like the violence witnessed in other parts of the South. There was neither a great deal of news coverage nor a great deal of public discussion about what was going on. Rev. Samuel Kyles, who was the chairman of the local NAACP's education committee at the time, noted that the decision to use first-graders instead of high school students was intentional. Kyles believed that first graders were not tainted and therefore were better suited to integrate the schools."* -
> *Wikipedia*

> *The story is told at: http://thememphis13.com/*

The best I can tell, Memphis Central High was integrated along with all the other Memphis schools in 1965, following the Civil Rights Act of 1964. That is the year I was in Viet Nam and the year we were married. Neither of us had a clue.

CHAPTER 9

The Boy Scouts and the Black Scout Camp

Harding College

My college registration pattern mirrored my Junior High pattern – one year in a Christian school, followed by the rest of the time in public school.

My dad was a great steward of his barbering money. He counted everything in terms of the number of haircuts it would take to pay for it. He saved some and he invested it in local real estate. He never talked about it and I never knew how many properties he owned, but when it came time for Cecil, and later, me to go to college, he never blinked – he paid the way. No scholarships, no federal loans. Just cash. Including a $20 bill in the mail every week for expenses and treats.

In September, 1959, it was time for me to go off to school. I packed one suitcase and shipped it to Searcy,

Arkansas, on a Greyhound Bus. That evening I got on my trusty Schwinn, one-speed, coaster-brake bike and peddled the 109 miles to Harding College. I went at night because it was cooler. It never occurred to me that a Black boy of my age could not have safely taken such a trip.

That first year of college was a mixed blessing for me. I had never met my roommate, Mike, before, but he and I became best buddies. In fact, as far as I remember, he was my only real friend. At the Christian school, Social Clubs took the place of fraternities and sororities. We pledged the Mohicans and because "Mohican" sounded like "Mohawk," we gave each other Mohawk haircuts. We were, of course, summoned to the Dean's office so that the ever-vigilant administration could satisfy itself that we were not being hazed and had not been compelled to cut our hair.

I thought I wanted to be a doctor. I am still not sure why. That entailed one five-hour math course that, once I changed my major, kept me from having to take any more math at all.

I spent most of my time that year with the drama club. I built a set for a one-act play that included a jail cell. The door had to open and close and the whole thing had to be portable because we were going to take the play to a nearby junior college. I built it alone from trashed lumber and plumbing, mostly at night.

I worked on a lot of sets and usually opened and closed the curtain. It was a heavy curtain that was counterbalanced and that rose out of sight. I did it with flair, raising it quickly and likewise closing it quickly making it stop just as it reached the floor. I was the best curtain handler they had seen in a while.

I even got a part in our one, big, three-act play of the year, Shakespeare's "King Lear." That whole thing was a fiasco, but is not particularly relevant here.

Mike and I got in trouble before the year was out. He actually had some other friends, people I didn't really know. Mike had not been involved, but his friends broke into a local drug store and stole some watches. They were about to get caught. Maybe they had been caught. They wanted to get rid of the watches so they asked Mike to make them disappear. Mike enlisted my help and we dropped them into a couple of storm sewers. Once again, I was going along to get along, a flaw I fight even today.

The next day we were summoned to the dean's office and confronted with what we had done. I never saw a police officer or even the thieves themselves, but we were suspended from school. One thing I learned from that experience was not to trust a group of thieves. The school let us finish the school year, but we were told we would have to reapply before we could come back the next fall.

Camp Yocona

Meanwhile my older brother had taken a position as a Boy Scout District Executive in northern Mississippi. That summer he was running the all-White Camp Yocona and he hired me to run the kitchen. There were two wonderful, well-loved, older, local women who did the cooking and told me what foodstuffs to order. My job included placing the orders, checking the deliveries, maintaining a form that calculated the price per camper for every meal and supervising the two dishwashers who were older local scouts who had been hired for the purpose.

Because of what I had learned about music at Union Avenue, I also fell into the song leader's role, which I carried out with great enthusiasm and acclaim. I learned to play the bugle and played all the calls: reveille, assembly, the calls to raise and lower the flag and taps. I worked at the camp all four summers of my college career.

Complex Me

The waterfront staff were the wannabe heroes of the camp. One day they had closed the waterfront - no swimming or working on aquatic merit badges - because of inclement weather. The sun had come out and the waterfront crew was still in their cabin. That summer we had a staff member who had a trombone, so I got him and two or three others and we marched down the hill to the waterfront cabin, the trombone playing and us singing the theme to the Micky Mouse Club: "M-I-C-K-E-Y M-O-U-S-E." The waterfront was open again in about ten minutes.

I tell that story to illustrate something of the complexity of my personality at the time. Compare that story to the one about the rafts on the Tallahatchee River in the next chapter

The Black Boy Scout Camp

At the end of the camping season there were always two or three weeks before school started and each year I did something different related to the Boy Scouts. That first summer the Regional Executive came out and asked if any of us would be willing to help at the Black camp. Not only were there no Black troops who came to Yocona, but there were no Black kids in any of the White troops either. There was a Black camp at a different location.

I don't know why, but I was the only volunteer. I never thought twice about it. I didn't spend any time debating the pros and cons, and neither my dad nor my brother and sister-in-law, who were my overseers in Mississippi at the time, expressed any concern. I am guessing it just seemed too different for the others. I never detected any racism from them.

The camp ran for two weeks, but I came down with the flu the first week. I was very disappointed, but I was better in time for the second week. It was 1960. I was the only White person in camp all week and was a junior staffer. My bosses and the campers I was teaching were all Black. I taught map reading, knot tying and how to lash poles together to make a bridge. The Black leaders treated me just like they did the other workers. I did not perceive that they gave me any deference.

At the White camp the kids all arrived as part of a troop, with their scout leaders in tow. At the Black camp the kids came individually and the camp provided around-the-clock supervision. I was assigned a cabin of young campers. There was one young boy who was afraid of the dark. He slept under my bed, thinking it would be safer there.

In my mind I was building a bridge between the races, but to my knowledge no one ever used the bridge I had built. I did not maintain contact with any of the scouts or with the leaders. But being the loner I was, I didn't maintain contact with anyone from high school or Harding either, not even my best friend, Mike.

During my other three years of college I am sure the opportunity to work at the Black camp would have still been there, but nothing was said about it and I had other choices – choices that put me with my White friends. I wonder what would have come of it, had I gone back to the Black camp three more times. Maybe I could have taken some of my White friends along.

CHAPTER 10

Ole Miss & The Tallahatchee River Again

That summer I became friends with several other camp workers, especially Jim Foster. Jim was a former Marine having served in Korea. That made him a few years older than the rest of us. He was a Boy Scout leader and spent his summers working at the camp. There was a small cadre of camp employees who were Jim's disciples and I joined the group. Jim was a master story teller and I wanted to hear more stories.

That fall I shifted my college choice to The University of Mississippi, "Ole Miss". I had to get permission from Harding to be readmitted before Ole Miss would accept me, but they were very gracious and granted me that favor.

There was a group of about five of us that spent the next two years in Jim's dorm room, drinking coffee from his bottomless percolator, talking about the Boy Scouts and listening to Jim's stories. Jim was a year ahead of me in school and was studying to be a schoolteacher – science, I believe. I changed my major to education and selected Social Studies as a subject, because that seemed like the easiest course to take. I didn't do a lot of studying – just got by, saving my time for the scouts and for our endless sessions in Jim's room.

Sometime while I was at Ole Miss, I read a book written by a New Orleans Juvenile Court Judge. It was just a collection of the stories of the children that had come before him in Juvenile Court. It changed the course of my life. I don't remember the title and have been unable to find it since.

Most of Jim's disciples signed on with the same scout troop he was with, but my independent streak drove me to join the leadership of a much smaller troop south of town, out in the boonies. I was the assistant scoutmaster and ran all the activities, just as Jim and his friends did with the larger troop in town.

Where is David?

There are hundreds of stories I could tell, but I will tell this one. It illustrates my propensity to go along to get along. It may help you understand who I am, or it may confuse you further as it did me.

We, Jim's disciples, were always dreaming up some kind of adventure for us and the scouts. One year we built two rafts. We took some used lumber and some empty 55-gallon oil drums and put them together in such a way that they floated. We built a rectangular platform, strapped a drum at each corner and launched them in the Tallahatchie River. You remember the Tallahatchie. That's where Emmettt Till's body was thrown after it was wired to the 74-pound gin fan.

We ran the river a couple of times with the scouts, pulling out at Batesville. As the weather was tapering off toward the Mississippi version of winter, two of my buddies, Roger and Terry, and I went to get the rafts out of the water. The water was high and fast. We tied the two rafts together and set off down river. About two thirds of the way to Batesville, the raft we were on got hung up on some tree limbs just under the surface of the water. Our raft had been in front and the back raft was drifting by. As it passed, I jumped to the empty raft thinking we should try to save it. The line holding them together snapped and I was going down river alone. I shouted back that I would come back for them.

When I got to the bridge over the river near Batesville I was able to negotiate the raft to the bank and climb up to the highway. I caught a ride into town and went to the sheriff's office, thinking he could help me go back for my friends. The problem was that the sheriff either didn't believe my story or was just too lazy to get out. He fed me dinner, took me back to the car I had come over in and told me to go home and get some rest, saying my friends had probably gotten out by then on their own.

Instead I cruised up and down the highways on either side of the river stopping and calling my friends' names. I ran into one man who offered to put his boat in the water for me, but I declined. I don't know why unless I just didn't want to put him out. That was perhaps the down side of my independent streak. Eventually, I gave up and went home to bed, thinking that Roger and Terry had gotten out on their own, like the sheriff had said.

Well, the next morning Roger called. He was livid that I had gone home and left them out there, and rightfully so. Roger had finally given up on me returning and risked the dangerous swim to shore. He went into town and found the Rescue Squad to go get Terry. I didn't even know there was such a thing as a Rescue Squad. Surely the sheriff did, but he never mentioned it. I apologized, but I probably did not ask them to forgive me. I don't believe they ever did.

Even today, I am not sure how to analyze this and what it says about me. Here are some random thoughts.

1. I was shy, especially around authority figures.
2. My confidence was strong in some matters, like leading the camp in song, but was weak in others, like when it came to something I interpreted as defying an authority figure.
3. These two factors were what drove my independent streak. I wanted to be on my own and to operate alone so I didn't have to deal with others.
4. The decision to go home that night has always been one of my greatest regrets. I can't imagine what possessed me.
5. But I did learn to second guess people in authority.

January 31, 1961 – Members of the Congress of Racial Equality (CORE) and nine students are arrested in Rock Hill, South Carolina, for a sit-in at a McCrory's lunch counter.

May 21, 1961 – Martin Luther King, the Freedom Riders, and a congregation of 1,500 at Rev. Ralph Abernathy's First Baptist Church in Montgomery were besieged by a mob of segregationists;

Robert F. Kennedy as Attorney General sent federal marshals to protect them.

September, 1961 – 13 Black first graders integrated Memphis City Schools.

CHAPTER 11

James Meredith and "Blowing in the Wind"

I was 20 years old at the beginning of our senior year. Jim had graduated, leaving us disciples on our own. We must have felt a little like the twelve did standing on that hilltop in Galilee when Jesus went home.

On Saturday night, September 29, 1962, a large group of U.S. Marshals rolled onto campus in Army trucks, accompanying a Black man, James Howard Meredith, to the registrar's office to be admitted to the all-White university. President Kennedy and Mississippi Governor, Ross Barnett, had been sparring for weeks. Federal courts overruled the state courts and ordered Meredith's admission. The Feds had threatened Barnett and his Lieutenant Governor with jail and a substantial daily fine until they allowed Meredith to be admitted. State Troopers had been on campus for several days, on Barnett's orders, to keep Meredith out.

I believe the Marshalls had chosen that Saturday night, thinking many of the students and school supporters would have been out of town at the Kentucky football game being played 160 miles away (by interstate) in Jackson – at least a three-hour drive at that time. What they didn't calculate was that the students would all be returning to campus, many of them drunk.

Meredith was in the Lyceum, the administration building. As you come onto the campus, the Lyceum is the first thing you see. In front of it is a large circular drive, University Circle. That circle has since been designated as a National Historic Landmark in honor of that night and there is a statue of James Meredith on one edge. The statue is of him walking toward an archway.

Two of my friends and I were on the south side of the circle, waiting to see what happened next. We had heard of Meredith's arrival on the news. Several Marshals were spread across the Lyceum porch. We were excited. History was being made and we believed it was right to admit Meredith to the University.

Soon the students returned and it turned ugly. They were standing around grumbling at first. Then one guy, dressed head to foot in a Confederate uniform from the ball game, got on top of a vehicle and started leading football cheers. The school mascot was "The Rebel" – a confederate soldier. Soon people started throwing rocks at the Marshals and then the Marshals got out the tear gas. University Circle was full of tear gas and it drifted in our direction, so we left.

One of the guys had an uncle who was a professor at the university, so we went to his house to watch the news.

At Dr. Tatum's house, we learned that there were units of the 101st Airborne Division flying into the Oxford airport, so we went out to watch. It was quite a sight – much like watching John Wayne and the cavalry show up at the last minute to rescue the settlers at the Memphian Theater on a Saturday afternoon, only in real life. You will remember the 101st from WW2 and the Little Rock 9. They were being delivered in C-130 aircraft, 4 engine prop jobs with reversible propellers.

The aircraft were ideal for landing on the super short Oxford runways because as soon as they touched the ground the pilot could reverse the pitch of the propellers and rev them up so that they were blowing in the opposite direction. They could stop like a horse wanting to rid of itself of its rider. As soon as one was clear, the next one was landing. It was a heady evening for a bunch of college students.

Just like the nine kids at Little Rock High, James Meredith was to be accompanied on his adventure by the nation's finest. He still, though, suffered many indignities. We heard tales of a dead racoon being placed on his Volkswagen, and I have read of students leaving the table when he tried to join them in the cafeteria. He was a brave man with a thick skin.

Years later a friend of mine in Florida told me the rest of the story. He was in the 82nd Airborne at the time. The 82nd was the other of the two divisions of paratroopers who dropped into southern France in the dark on D-Day when the allied troops were attacking Normandy Beach on June 6, 1944.

When James Meredith was brought to Ole Miss by the Marshals, the 82nd was positioned at the Millington Naval Air Station just north of Memphis. Their orders, were they to be called on to execute them, were to parachute onto the grounds of the State Capitol in Jackson Mississippi and occupy the capitol building. Kennedy wasn't playing games with Barnett.

I just had the rest of that semester left on campus, but that doesn't excuse my inactivity. I could have befriended him. I did once, in the library, sit down beside him for a couple of minutes and tell him that there were lots of students on campus who supported his right to be there. He thanked me and, graciously, he didn't bring up the fact that we all were too frightened to show our colors. But it is significant, I think, that there was never any debate among my friends, the Jim Foster disciples, about whether James Meredith belonged there. We all knew he did.

Speaking of colors, just so you have a bit of a feel for the tone of the campus, the school band owned a huge Confederate flag, so large that it stretched from side to side on the football field and most of the field's length. Once each year, probably at homecoming, they would break it out. The band would spread out on the field with "T" shaped poles and would completely cover the band with the flag, while they played Dixie, all the time using the poles to poke at the flag overhead so it waved. The crowd went into uncontrollable hysterics.

Now you do need to understand that the Rebel flag to most White folks at the time was not especially about Black people. It was about cotton fields and thunderstorms and fried chicken and corn bread and people in D.C. telling us what to do.

I do know that those things are seen very differently by Black people. The White folk were just not thinking about that. In fact, for many of us, that may be our greatest sin – not thinking.

The rest of the semester the local radio station constantly played Peter, Paul and Mary's version of Bob Dylan's tune, "Blowing in the Wind." I have often wondered about that White DJ and his management who kept putting that song forward on the Oxford radio station: "Yes, and how many years can a mountain exist before it is washed to the sea? Yes, and how many years can some people exist before they're allowed to be free?"

I still tear up when I hear that song, especially the last lines: "Yes and how many times can a man turn his head and pretend that he just doesn't see? The answer, my friend, is blowing in the wind. The answer is blowing in the wind."

And speaking of tearing up, decades ago I had a Joan Baez 33 1/3 vinyl album that included "We Shall

Overcome." I played it when no one else was around to see me cry. And I have always loved "I Shall Not Be Moved." That one is even in some of our church songbooks. I have led it on Sunday morning a few times, but it is just not the same when it is sung by a room full of White people. I played it this morning. Found it done by a group of kids, Black and White. I was in tears when Charlene came into the room. The verses "Hand in hand together" and "Black and White together" especially get to me.

James Meredith and I graduated from the same school at the same time in 1963. That's my claim to fame.

> *June 11, 1963 – "The Stand in the Schoolhouse Door": Alabama Governor George Wallace stood in front of a schoolhouse door at the University of Alabama in an attempt to stop desegregation by the enrollment of two black students.*
>
> *June 12, 1963 – NAACP worker Medgar Evers was murdered in Jackson, Mississippi. His killer was convicted in 1994 [31 years later].*

S

CHAPTER 12

The USMC; Charlene; and the Buffalo

Continuing to follow in Jim's footsteps, I joined the Marine Corps. It was one of my better moves. I signed up during my junior year at Ole Miss and was held in the "Inactive Reserve" until graduation. After graduation, I did one last summer of Boy Scout work, then escorted a gang of Explorer Scouts (14 and older) to the Boundary Waters Canoe Area in northern Minnesota and Canada. My best memory from that trip was going first through the cafeteria line and telling the cashier that the next seventeen were mine. That and telling one kid that one more infraction and I would put him on a plane for home, at his momma's expense, and meaning it.

> *On August 28, 1963, Martin Luther King gave his "I Have a Dream" speech during the march on Washington.*

As September approached I bought a motorcycle and rode it to Quantico, Virginia. Motorcycles were not allowed at the Marine Corps' Officer Candidate School (OCS), so I stored it at my cousin's apartment near DC where he was, I think, working for the CIA. Officially, though, he was in the Army and assigned to the Pentagon.

> *September 10, 1963 – Birmingham, Alabama, City Schools are integrated by National Guardsmen under orders from President Kennedy.*

Meanwhile, terrorism continued right here in the states:

> *On September 15, 1963, the 16th Street Baptist Church was bombed in Birmingham, killing four little girls.*

OCS was about thirteen weeks of screening out the misfits. At times, I suspected I was one, but deep down I knew I wasn't. I knew God and Charlene were on my side, and nobody could beat that combination.

There were lots of fun OCS stories, but they are not particularly relevant here.

In summary, I will say that I was never an athlete. The closest I ever came to playing sports was manning the down markers for Junior High football. And I had some trouble climbing the ropes. On the other hand, I knew how to march and how to drill the platoon, and I was a determined runner. Somehow a rumor spread that I had run cross-country in college. Nothing could have been further from the truth. What I did during the runs was ask God to help me and think about how disappointed Charlene would be if I got culled.

From time to time the drill instructors would call one guy out of formation and we would never see him again. When we got back to the barracks that night, his gear would all be gone and his mattress would be rolled up on the bed.

One day they called my name. They took me into the office and told me that I was not going to make it, but I knew better. I was doing well academically, had been one of a small group who had finished a surprise test run, had bested my opponent in pummeling each other with padded sticks, and had frequently been called on to drill the platoon. By then I had them figured out. They were testing our resolve under duress.

When it was all over, each platoon's drill instructors chose an outstanding cadet to get a free dress blue uniform. They chose an exceptional guy who had been an enlisted Marine and was one of the few who are chosen from the ranks to go to OCS. But our Sergeant took me aside and told me that he and the other drill instructors had wanted me to have the honor. The Captain had wanted it to be a former enlisted man. I was prouder of being selected by the drill instructors than I would have been to be chosen by the Captain.

At the end of OCS, we all were given our gold bars, became 2nd Lieutenants and, for the first time, were called "Marines". Then we went through six months of "The Basic School", the first of a series of leadership schools for officers. I don't remember any Black guys being there. It was a pretty white Marine Officers Corps. I think that lasted until things heated up in Viet Nam.

> *June 9, 1964 – Bloody Tuesday – peaceful marchers were beaten, arrested and tear gassed by Tuscaloosa, Alabama police on a peaceful march to the County Courthouse to*

protest whites-only restroom signs and drinking fountains.

June 21, 1964 – Chaney, Goodman, and Schwerner, three civil rights workers disappeared from Philadelphia, Mississippi and were later found murdered and buried in an earthen dam.

In the Summer of 1964, following Basic School, I got a break to go home. Our younger brother, Charlie, fifteen at the time, came up to Quantico and we took my old Pontiac to New York to the 1964 World's Fair. From there we headed for home until somewhere in the Carolinas the Pontiac quit forever. I sold it for scrap, got the motorcycle out of the back seat and we finished the trip on it.

Charlene

When I got home, I had a few weeks before reporting to Camp Pendleton in California for training, then on to my first duty station in Okinawa. Viet Nam was not yet in our common vocabulary. We knew something was going on over there, but the U.S. was not officially involved, at least not at a level that a brand new 2nd Lieutenant would know about.

When I was home on this break, Charlene was in nursing school at the University of Tennessee, staying in the dorm. For the first time, ever, if I wanted to see her, I had to call and ask for a date. She claims I was wrong, but I believed that if I went to Okinawa for thirteen months, she would be engaged or married to one of the med students at the University when I returned.

I didn't really understand dating protocols, but I invited her to go downtown to see "Old Yeller." When the movie was over, I was going to drop her off at the dorm. It seemed natural enough to me, but apparently it was a serious breach of protocol.

She asked me to come in for a minute, left me in the "visitation" room and went to her dorm room. She came back with a greeting card my older brother had helped her pick out. It seems everyone but me knew about our situation.

The front of the card said, "Our relationship must be perfectly clear to you by now." Inside, the card read, "Would you mind explaining it to me?" I chuckled and said I needed to think about it. A few nights later I proposed and she said "yes." There is much more to that story, but not for this book.

The short form of my Marine Corps stint is this: Charlene and I were engaged for fifteen months and were together ten days of that. We had had one date, but had lived in the same house for eighteen months. Our oldest son, years later, told his friends at the Christian university he attended that his parents lived together before they were married. Then after a dramatic pause would say, "But that's okay, they were brother and sister." You may need to stop and think about that one.

December 10, 1964 – Dr. King was awarded the Nobel Peace Prize, the youngest person so honored.

I did six weeks of training at Camp Pendleton, California; then reported to my duty station in Okinawa where I was assigned as the platoon leader of a platoon of 39 Marines and 11 Amtracs. An Amtrac is an amphibious, ship-to-shore tracked vehicle, 10 feet high, 30 feet long, weighing 36 tons, empty. One will carry 36 Marines in full battle gear. It takes some courage to drive one off a Navy ship. They typically sink to a point where about 12 inches of its 10 foot height is above the water. It has powerful bilge pumps and when it is in the water it is often shooting water high into the air from all four corners.

From Okinawa we set out to sea a couple of times. The first time, my unit was attached to a battalion that was about due to go home. We sat on our ships in the Da Nang, Viet Nam, harbor, while another identical unit went ashore - the first official combat Marines to go to Viet Nam. We went back to Okinawa, were attached to the replacement troops for the units that went home and we went back to Da Nang to go ashore.

Most of the bridges had been blown up by then by one side or the other, so the only two ways for troops to move around were helicopter and Amtrac. We were pretty busy. My platoon was stationed away from the rest of the Amtracs at a river crossing, the site where a bridge had been.

Looking at our platoon picture, there were five Black Marines out of a platoon of 39. The sergeants had much closer interaction with the troops than I did, but they kept me well informed. I never heard of any inter-racial difficulties.

> *March 7, 1965 – Bloody Sunday: Civil rights workers in Selma, Alabama, began the Selma to Montgomery march but were attacked and stopped by a massive Alabama State trooper and police blockade as they crossed the*

Edmund Pettus Bridge into the county. Many marchers were injured.

August 11–15, 1965 – Following accusations of mistreatment and police brutality by the Los Angeles Police Department towards the city's African-American community, Watts riots erupted in South Central Los Angeles and lasted over five days. Over 34 were killed, 1,032 injured, 3,438 arrested, and there was over $40 million in property damage.

The Marine Corps lost my rotation card two months in a row, so my thirteen-month tour lasted fifteen months. We scheduled the wedding first in October, then in November and, at the end, I wired home on a Sunday that I would be there Saturday in time for the wedding. I arrived Tuesday evening and we were married the following Saturday night, November 13, 1965, my 24th birthday.

Jim Foster and another of his disciples, Win Davis, were in the wedding. My brother performed the ceremony. At the reception the entire group sang "Happy Birthday" as Charlene and I entered the reception hall.

Jim and Win gave us a full-sized buffalo hide from a herd on the Philmont Scout Ranch in New Mexico.

From there for the next forty years or so we had the dilemma of what to do with a buffalo hide. It eventually found its way to my office and graced one whole wall.

The Boy Scouts during this time period used a lot of stories and Native American dress and paraphernalia as a part of their rituals. They considered it honoring of the culture and sometimes brought in local Native American people to explain various items and to tell stories. Some have called it cultural appropriation and labeled it as disrespectful. If I were going back to those days, I would want to do some more research before I engaged.

After the wedding I had one more year of my obligation to the Marine Corps. We went to the Cherry Point Marine Corps Air Station in Havelock, North Carolina, and enjoyed a year-long honeymoon. There I made the rank of Captain.

> *June 5, 1966 – James Meredith began a solitary March Against Fear from Memphis, Tennessee to Jackson, Mississippi. Shortly after starting, he was shot with birdshot and injured. Civil rights leaders and organizations rallied and continued the march. This led to, on June 16, Stokely Carmichael first using the*

slogan "Black Power" in a speech. Twenty-five thousand marchers entered the capital.

Chapter 13

Delinquent Kids and Toilet Seats

Prompted by the Juvenile Judge's book, my first gig out of the Marines was as an "Aftercare Counselor" for the State of Florida. That is a juvenile parole officer, doing home studies for kids being sent away to one of the state's large institutions for juveniles and supervising them when they came home. We moved to Cocoa, Florida, and opened a new one-person field office there. Sounds exotic and it was.

My two-county jurisdiction included Cape Canaveral (later Cape Kennedy) where the launching pads for the Apollo Space Program were located. Moms and dads were working night and day and were making tons of money while the kids ran up and down the beaches, raising themselves. We lived there one year and welcomed the birth of our first son, Mike.

One of the kids I was charged with keeping up with was a skinny little nine-year-old Black boy who had previously been sent off to the training school for shoplifting. He was back in court, accused of taking something from a store without paying. There were four of us in the courtroom that day: the judge, the county's probation officer (acting as prosecutor), the boy, and me.

They had spoken of the charge, but there were no witnesses, no evidence presented, just the prosecutor's report. The boy spoke with a heavy southern Black dialect.

Judge: "Have you heard of the 10 commandments?"

Boy: "Yassah."

Judge: "Do you know where they are found?"

Boy: "Yassah."

Judge: "Where is that?"

Boy: "Exo-das 11. Verses 3-20"

The judge, of course, was expecting him to say it was found in the Bible or that he didn't know. The little boy was the only person in the room who knew the chapter and verse.

Being new to the scene, I mentioned the fact that no evidence had been presented and, by the way, the boy had said he didn't steal the candy bar or whatever it was. The judge chuckled, pointed out for the record that "Mr. May says you are innocent until proven guilty," and ordered the little boy returned to the Florida School for Boys in Marianna. That's where the thugs and gangsters from Jacksonville were sent. That was my introduction to juvenile justice in Florida.

FSBO

I worked for the State of Florida for 25 years. An early part of that, right after I went to Florida State University to get my Master's Degree, was as the Social Services Director for the Florida School for Boys at Okeechobee. FSBO was out in the boonies and served Miami and the southern third of the state. I was sent there by the headquarters in Tallahassee. I think I was supposed to be some kind of reformer. While we were there, our second son, Mark, was born.

> *April 4, 1968 – Martin Luther King, Jr. is shot and killed in Memphis, Tennessee.*

The junior campus manager, “Mr. G”, was a salty old guy who surreptitiously carried a billy club. The rumor was that he used it a lot on the kids, which was not only against the rules, but was also illegal. As the social service director, my staff and I got the worst of the stories, which we documented.

Eventually I handed the whole set of papers, several inches thick, over to the Superintendent, but addressed to his boss in Tallahassee, knowing the local Superintendent was not going to do anything. Soon the Superintendent took a vacation and the big guy from the State Capitol came down to sit in for him for a few days. I pointed out the package addressed to him on the Superintendent’s desk.

Nothing of significance that I could see ever came of our documentation, though I do believe Mr. G retired not too long after. I was bitterly disappointed that more was not made of this ongoing, illegal mistreatment of the boys at the school and of the fact that the Superintendent had ignored it for years.

I had considered turning the package over to the local Grand Jury, to the newly formed Florida Department of Law Enforcement (the State Police), or to the Miami Herald. But, like a good state employee, I sent them up the chain of command instead. I went along to get along. The only satisfaction I ever got from all that documentation was that when I accepted a promotion to the Program Director's position at the larger, older institution in Marianna, the Okeechobee Superintendent told the Marianna Superintendent, "Watch your back."

Integration, Florida Style

One of my friends at Okeechobee was a young Jewish houseparent from Miami, named Jerry. Most of the house parents were older, local guys. Jerry had been there longer than me or any of my staff and he told a story about the integration of the school a few years earlier.

Before integration, there was a Black campus and a White campus with a very large green space in between. Mr. G, the thug with the billy club, had been in charge of the Black campus and his responsibility was to see that no one in the main office ever had to deal with the Black kids. He accomplished that successfully with the billy club and various other forms of violent, abusive treatment.

The first level of integration at the school was to move cottages of Black kids to the White Campus, and vice versa, creating new "Junior" and "Senior" campuses.

Jerry was so stricken by the sight of the transfer that he told us the story repeatedly. He told of large groups of Black kids crossing the green commons with their toilet seats around their necks and groups of White kids going the other way in like fashion.

Though about half of the staff at both schools were Black, the administration was so corrupt in both places that they should have been shut down. The Superintendent at Marianna was such a drunk that he fell down at a conference we had with another, private school and had to be helped to his room. He was an embarrassment to the State, but they wouldn't do anything about it.

Chapter 14

Sadly, Back to Union Avenue

I continued to work for the State of Florida until 1987, eventually serving as the Child Welfare Administrator for the state, working out of the headquarters in Tallahassee, the state's capitol city.

At some time during that period, we went looking for our old church back in Memphis. We were very disappointed that White Flight had caused the church to move. As Black people moved into areas that had previously been all White, many White people moved out. In the case of Memphis, that meant they moved mostly east and south.

There was actually a subdivision south of Memphis formally named White Haven. The husband of one of my stepsisters was a preacher in that town. In fact, the church where he preached was called the "White

Haven Church of Christ." I had dinner there and sometimes passed through there on my way to Oxford. Only in the last few years has it dawned on me what the name meant. Why wasn't I better tuned in? I don't know.

Once most of the Union Avenue congregation had moved out of the area, the church sold the building to a Black church. Only in the last few weeks have we gone back to the old building to visit the Midtown Church of Christ. They are doing very well without the White members who sold out and moved east. But I can't help think of the good that could have been done had the White people stayed and welcomed their new Black neighbors.

To Charlene and me, that move represented giving in to racism. They sold the building to a church of the same faith, and that church still meets there today, but the White church is nowhere near. The old Union Avenue building was walking distance from the home in which I grew up and the elementary school I attended. It hurt to know that the leaders of our old church had chosen to abandon the area rather than stay and gracefully help shepherd in the changes as our Black brothers and sisters joined with us..

I feel I have earned the right to criticize Union Avenue because of all they taught me in the earlier years. Love your neighbor and all that.

We never lived in Memphis after we were married and, whenever we were there, we were busy visiting family. I am not sure when Union Avenue sold the building and moved, but it was after both our parents were dead. That would most likely make it in the 1990s or later.

We went to visit with the new church, now under a different name much further east. It looked quite ordinary, very suburban-like. The old Union Avenue building is huge and stately.

After a very ordinary service, we stayed for a dinner the congregation graciously offered to visitors. A man was there, now a leader, whom we had known when he was a young man, years before. During the dinner, the man made a very racist comment, thereby confirming our thought about the nature of the group. I am just grateful that neither our parents nor either of us was there to witness the transition. May God bless the Midtown congregation meeting in the old Union Avenue building and may He teach and redirect the group who moved away.

Chapter 15

The Minnesota Years

In 1987 we moved to Minnesota. By then we were six in number. Charlene had given birth to three boys, Michael, Mark and Matt, and we had adopted a girl, Jennifer, when she was seven. We were still, at that point, an all-White family. Matt was born in 1973 during a sojourn in Orlando, between Marianna and Tallahassee. Jennifer's story is in Chapter 18.

At first, we were thinking we would move back to Florida in two or three years, so we held on to the nice house we had built in the country near Capitola. My dad had added a big room to it to stay in until his colon cancer finished its course. It had three other bedrooms plus a sleeping loft I had built. Because all our equity was tied up in Florida, we bought a rather small (for us) house in a second ring Saint Paul suburb. Our kids finished school while we were there.

Eventually, though too late to be advantageous taxwise, I gave up on capturing my dream job in Florida, and we sold the Florida house. Then we had enough money to move into Saint Paul and pursue my latest dream: an “urban ministry”.

By the time we moved into the city, we were down to one son at home and his son, our grandson, Alex. We bought a large house, almost 100 years old, on the West Side of Saint Paul. It was a beautiful place and Charlene declared to our realtor when we discovered it that it was her dream home. We soon set out to found what we called the “Saint Paul Urban Ministry” (SPUM).

The Saint Paul Urban Ministry

We were members of the suburban Woodbury Church of Christ at the time and I was one of two elders there. I had a vision for SPUM that was very different from what God had in mind. He was leading at every step. As we look back, we can see His hand at every part of our lives, especially in the big decisions.

And I cannot tell the Urban Ministry story without an emphasis on how God worked in it.

I envisioned a downtown Saint Paul church made up of some homeless town people and some commuters who lived in the suburbs and worked downtown.

Our son, Mark, (#2 son) was the youth minister at the Oxford, Mississippi, Church of Christ. Oxford is home to Ole Miss. I had been talking about the urban ministry and Mark called to ask if we could use a summer intern in it. At this point, our inner-city work was just a dream, but I said "yes" and soon Richard Palmer, a Black man, joined our team. Or should I say became our team. Richard had been a classmate of Mark's at Magnolia Bible College in Kosciusco, Mississippi, where Mark had recently graduated and where my brother, Cecil, was the president. Kosciusco, a small county seat, by the way, is the birthplace of both James Meredith and Oprah Winfrey. We drove past the home Oprah grew up in when we were there on a visit.

Richard lived with us and we fed him. He had a very small allowance from his home congregation where his father was the preacher. That was his compensation for the summer. He had done two previous summer internships with urban ministries, one in Nashville and one in Atlanta. Both had been aimed at Black, inner city children.

Richard and Charlene recruited several of the Woodbury church ladies and a couple of guys to volunteer to teach kids Bible stories that they may not have ever heard before. Richard got us a free room in The Neighborhood House, a community center on the edge of Dunedin, a public housing complex in Saint Paul. It was about a 15-minute walk from where we lived. At that time, Dunedin was almost completely occupied by Hmong people, with White families and Black families in the single digits. The "H" is silent in Hmong.

The Hmong

The Hmong people are a story in and of themselves. The short form is this. They had never had a home country. They were in China for a few centuries and survived by staying in the mountains. By the time of the Viet Nam war, many of them had migrated into the mountains of Laos.

The U.S. wanted to maintain the appearance of not operating in Laos during the war, so the CIA secretly recruited the Hmong people to operate there as mercenaries on our behalf, interrupting the North

Vietnamese supply lines. When the U.S. pulled out of the war, the Laotian government targeted the Hmong for annihilation and the Hmong who survived fled across the Mekong River into Thailand. There, they were placed in refugee camps.

Eventually the U.S. Congress recognized the important role the Hmong people had played in the war and granted them refugee status in the United States. The largest concentration of Hmong people in the U.S. is found in refugee-friendly Minnesota.

At that time, most of the Hmong children had been born in the refugee camps in Thailand. A few of the older ones had been born earlier in Laos. Very few of the parents spoke English. The children were learning English quickly in school, creating awkward family dynamics, with the kids interpreting everything from school reports to medical information and financial data to be shared with the welfare office.

This role reversal in refugee families will often result in the children becoming extremely rebellious, but it did not play out that way with our families. In fact, I think there was something about the Hmong culture that offset that result. They have a very high regard for their elders.

That respect could have worked against our efforts to teach the children about Jesus, but it didn't. The mothers, who had complete control of the children, were very helpful to us. We were invited to what we would call potluck dinners, and the children were given wide latitude to participate in our activities.

The Urban Ministry

It all began when Richard and I made up some half-sheet flyers. In the afternoon at Dunedin, the kids were all outside. There were two playgrounds on the complex and many of the children were there. On Monday afternoons, Richard and I would go out and pass out the fliers announcing our "Kids' Connection" the next afternoon. The first Tuesday we met, about twenty kids showed up. Several of the eight or nine-year-old girls were carrying a baby on their hip because it was their responsibility to care for the little ones.

Our typical afternoon included a review of the previous week's story, raucous songs, a new story, snacks, and a craft related to the story. The craft was important for several reasons, including that it was something they could take home to show their mothers and tell them what was going on. Two birds:

one rock. The weekly attendance continued at about twenty.

The first summer after we started, we put three of the little girls – maybe 10 years old – on the bus to our church camp. None of us went along. The kids' English was imperfect at best. They were not familiar with American food, and had no idea what to expect.

At the end of the camp, the girls were asked what they wished were different about the week. They wished for more rice, so the next year the camp ladies cooked more rice, though not the kind of rice the girls had in mind.

Soon Mark called again and asked if we would like to have a southern youth group come up and do a Vacation Bible School. We accepted; Woodbury provided food and lodging; and, not having a church building close by, the Oxford youth did it on a green hillside between the housing project and the next-door elementary school.

Then a man from Kosciusco came to Minnesota for surgery. They went to church with us and came home to share a meal before going on down to the Mayo Clinic in Rochester, Minnesota, for the surgery. During lunch, we talked about the urban ministry. We didn't hear any more from him until a few weeks later when he called us from Mississippi and asked if we could use funds for a full-time minister. God works in amazing ways!

After one false start, we hired Steve and Tina Countryman who were ideal for the role. They came from working in Thailand. Steve had always wanted to work with kids and Tina had always wanted to work with people from Southeast Asia.

In the earliest days of the ministry, after we discovered that nearly all of our kids were Hmong, we went looking for more information. One of the stops Charlene and I made was at a local Lutheran church to see the pastor assigned to work with the Hmong people. He advised us against pursuing the effort. He said the culture was too strong. He told us that the kids would come for a while, but would eventually fade away and that would be that.

Twenty years later, the Saint Paul Urban Ministry has several staff members. Many of the original kids are now grown and are still participating with their own children. There is also a new work is going with a different set of children at another housing project. God obviously had an interest in introducing this new Asian group to the story of His Son.

In just a few years, those little camping pioneers have been succeeded by a Hmong week at the camp. Other kids are there too, but there are about 20 Hmong kids at the camp.

To further our knowledge, Steve, Tina, Charlene and I started attending an annual series of conferences on urban ministry. Before too many years, though, we learned that the focus of the urban ministry people on what they knew as the "inner city" was not particularly relevant to our work with Hmong people, so we switched to an annual international missions conference.

I have read some criticism of the "Inner City" works, particularly of places where it was White led, but it is not my intent to address that here.

Black Adoption

One year to the day after moving to Minnesota, I was promoted to the position of Social Services Director for Ramsey County. It was a fun job at first. It entailed overseeing public social services to seniors, people with developmental disabilities, and children. The children's services included child protection, foster care and adoption.

The adoption of U.S. foster children has always taken a backseat in the public's mind to the adoption of babies from around the world. By focusing on our foster children, we were able to set an all-time record for their adoption.

Art Treadwell was a young Black man who kept running into difficulty in his work in the Planning Office. My guess was that they didn't like his advocacy for Black issues. I asked to have him transferred to my supervision and assigned him a number of objectives, one of which was increasing the numbers of Black foster children who were being adopted.

With help from the state department of Human Services, Art established an African American Adoption Program (AAAP) and increased the adoption of Black children significantly. They gave me a plaque that reads "In recognition for your support to promote permanent families for our children." I am proud of that one. It still hangs on my wall, along with two diplomas and a 25-year plaque for service to the State of Florida.

The Civil Rights Museum

We had left Michael, our oldest, behind when we moved to Minnesota. He joined the rest of us after he finished his degree from Harding University. By finishing a degree at Harding, I suppose he finished what Charlene and I had only started there so many years earlier. For different reasons we both started in a Christian school and finished in a public school. I transferred to Ole Miss after one year and she transferred to the University of Tennessee Nursing College in Memphis to pursue a nursing degree.

All of our kids were now in Minnesota. Our extended family (my brother, Charlene's siblings and various cousins) were still down south. On one of our trips south, we stopped at the National Civil Rights Museum in Memphis. What struck me most about the museum was the quote on the plaque by the front door. As you may know, the museum is partly in what was the Lorraine Motel where Dr. King was assassinated four and a half years after his "I have a dream" speech. The quote is from the Biblical account of what Joseph's brothers said about him when they undertook to kill him, mostly because they didn't like the content of his dreams about them. The plaque is simply a quote from Genesis 37:19-20:

> *"Here comes this dreamer! Now then, come and let us kill him and throw him into one of*

the pits… Then let us see what will become of his dreams!"

Chapter 16

Haiti

Years earlier I had developed an interest in Haiti, the poorest country in this hemisphere. It started on our first, one-year, sojourn in Tallahassee in 1968 when we moved there to get my Master's Degree. Our church was getting a series of letters from a Haitian preacher, telling of his work and asking for help. I did some research and corresponded with him some during that year. That was that, except that I kept up with Haiti somewhat in the news.

Years later when we moved to Minnesota, I determined to learn more about Haiti. It was about the same time we began exploring the urban ministry idea, so I am thinking that something within me was waking up to the needs around us. About that time, I began to think more about Jesus' picture of the judgment in Matthew 25 wherein he separates those he is going to save from the others based on how they treated people who needed help.

We learned of a California-based effort that had been founded by a church youth group who were working in northern Haiti. In 1993 we made our first trip there. We made another trip while we were living in Minnesota, then we moved back to Florida from 2001 through 2005. Since that time, between the two of us we have made over 30 trips to Haiti.

Our experiences in Haiti and what we learned there would make a book series. While I am writing this book, Charlene is three feet to my right writing a biography of Roberta Edwards, an amazing woman we met there. Her book, entitled Roberta: Joy and Courage in a Clay Jar, Too Soon Broken, will be a much better source of information about Haiti and what we have learned from the Haitian people than anything I could write.

Let me say this about Roberta. She was Black and the daughter of a United States Marine. It is insufficient to say that her dad, Robert, had to put up with a lot of abuse on his way up through the Marine Corps ranks, eventually making Lieutenant Colonel before he retired.

Roberta moved to Haiti as a young woman and lived there the rest of her life, raising over 25 Haitian children in her own home and feeding 150 more in the nutrition center on her property.

Roberta was truly an amazing woman, dedicated to God and to the people of Haiti. She was a dear friend. On October 10, 2015, she was shot and killed on her way to buy gas for one of her vehicles. She was targeted. The shooting was not random. One of her younger children was kidnapped during the same incident, but there was never any demand for ransom. Roberta's murder was a major blow to everyone who knew of her work and especially to those who worked alongside her.

Charlene and I lived in Haiti for about two years in 2012-2014. We managed a guesthouse for mission groups, including medical teams, educational teams, and others. We were just a few blocks from Roberta where we often spent an evening sharing a devotional and having dinner with her and the kids. The kids frequently spent an evening with us as well, having dinner and playing games.

The Haitian people tend to see Americans and White people in general as potential sources of funding. Most of the White people they have met have been missionaries or employees of non-profit organizations. Haitians are generally polite, but they really don't trust White people. They have been promised a lot by White people who then go away and forget about them. White adults have off-handedly told some of the children they wanted to adopt the child and take them back to America. The children were bitterly disappointed when nothing came of it.

Adoption of Haitian children is extremely time-consuming, very expensive and tremendously frustrating. We have known families who have been working toward an adoption for several years and seem to be no further along now, after spending fortunes. The process is similar to the Haitian customs process in that every Haitian official who gets involved wants a lot of money to do his or her part, regardless of how miniscule that part may be. And when they do it, they will come up with something else they need to do, with an additional fee.

But we adopted a young Haitian boy through a different process.

Chapter 17

Ricky

While I was working In West Palm Beach, our agency partnered with a local TV station to feature a different kid each day during adoption week in February. By heightening the public awareness of the children needing adoption and by awakening and retraining our local adoption unit, we were able to repeat the record-breaking numbers of adoptions of foster children we had seen in Ramsey County, Minnesota.

The hand of God was clearly on this situation as well. Each day, the TV station would tease the next day's adoptable kid by showing a short video. Then on that child's day they would continue to run teasers all day and would run a longer feature of the child during the evening news.

During the second year's adoption week, our sister-in-law, Susan, was visiting us. She became aware of what the TV station was doing and, because she had formerly done foster care, wanted to know more. I remembered that the station - after the previous year's adoption week was over - had put together a video of all the clips. So, I brought it home for us to watch.

One of the children was Ricky, a nine-year-old Black boy. We knew, because of the nature of my work, that boys were harder to place for adoption than girls, that children over about four or five were harder to place, and older Black boys had no chance at all.

The TV crew presented Ricky as a baseball player. It turned out he was not, but he had played a little while he was in his most recent group home. When they got down to the interview, Ricky was standing outside and said that he wanted a forever home. Then he looked away from the camera, then back at it and said, "A Christian family."

Understand that in our early 60s we were empty nesters and were thoroughly enjoying it, but Charlene turned to me and said, "What are we going to do about that?" The next day we contacted the local foster care agency to see if this boy was still available. As expected, he was, and we started the process.

Since I was the boss in Palm Beach County we had to work through a neighboring county to get our training and to have our home study done. One of the earlier steps in the process was for the agency to give us more information about Ricky.

As it turned out he was really Ricardo Jean Pierre and was Haitian. As the story went, his mother had moved to the states and had left him behind with his grandmother in Haiti. But his grandmother died.

He had an aunt in the States who traveled to Haiti and brought Ricky back to live with his mother. This was before TSA came along and, according to the social services agency, the two-year-old was smuggled into Miami in a carry-on. Ricky remembers being in a very small, dark space.

Ricky's mother did not want him. Some social workers came around and signed him up for Head Start, but she wouldn't send him. When they came back and asked her why, she said he would never be worth anything anyway. He slept in a closet and was only allowed to eat whatever was left after the other kids were finished.

Eventually the state terminated his mother's rights and freed him for adoption. Nothing is known about his father, but whenever I run into someone with the last name of Jean Pierre in Haiti, I wonder.

Ricky was nine when the video was made and ten when we started the adoption process.

At about 12 years of age, at his request, I made him some business cards that said simply, "Ricky will work" and gave some examples. He went door to door handing out the cards and in a day or two he had all the work he could handle - mowing lawns, walking dogs, washing cars and boats – doing whatever people wanted done. He was a hard and faithful worker and always kept his appointments.

His school years in Florida were hard. Racism among elementary and middle school kids is vicious. The White kids didn't like him because he is Black. As a Haitian, he is very dark. But the African-American kids didn't like him, either, because he is Haitian. In south Florida, Haitians are at the very bottom of the social totem pole. That was hard for all of us.

The last thing Florida had known of Haitians was that the big sugar companies brought in large groups of them when it was time to cut the sugar cane. The companies put them up in slave-style concrete huts, sold them basics in the company store at high prices, paid them very little and returned them to Haiti after the crops were harvested. The system was similar to the sharecropper system in place throughout the south after slavery was abolished. They were technically "free," but owed the company so much that they functioned as slaves. When social advocates and the media put too much pressure on the sugar companies, they invented huge machines to replace the Haitian cutters.

Ricky's name, "Ricardo Jean Pierre", called out during roll call, gave him away as did the very dark color of his skin. One of the blessings of his adoption was the change of his name. I home-schooled him for two years after I retired, but he went back to public school to finish his education and get his diploma.

He is now living in Tampa, working full time for Apple, dabbling at creating his own clothing line and is about to go back to finish his college education. He is a good kid and a hard worker – a good looking young man

.

Chapter 18

Mick, Cordell and Phoenix

Our adopted daughter was originally named Jennifer. That's the name her birth mother wanted her to have. When our third son was born, had he been a girl, we would have named her Jennifer. For several years, Charlene and I and the boys had talked about the Jennifer that would come along some day.

Eventually Charlene came to believe that the world was not a good enough place to bring more children into it. And I was really pushing adoption of foster children in my position with the State of Florida. So, we signed up.

In a process that went much too fast, we adopted Jennifer through a private agency in central Florida.

The state had very recently gotten the seven-year-old's mother to give up her rights. They had not made any progress in getting Jenn to accept that fact.

The five of us drove from Tallahassee to Gainesville to meet Jennifer. During the introduction, the foster father, in giving her an instruction, used a derogatory term to refer to her, alerting me that this was not a particularly good place for her." We took her out to eat and we all spent that first night with long-time friends of ours. The next day Jennifer went home with us.

Anyone who knows anything about adoption processes would know that was way too fast for everybody. I should have blown the whistle, but once again, I did not. I went along to get along.

Based on her mother's telling of the events, young Jennifer became convinced that the state had stolen her from her mother whom she loved dearly. That is not the best way to start a relationship.

Jennifer changed her name through the years and is now known as Mick. She married a little older than the average, but to an exceptional man. Cordell loves her dearly and is very kind and gentle. He is Black. They had a delightful wedding, themed after "The Princess

Bride", with the wedding party and guests dressed as their favorite fantasy or fairy tale character.

In the summer of 2017, Mick gave birth to a wonderful little boy named Phoenix.

Chapter 19

Our Family Now

After our five-year return to Florida from 2001 through 2005, we moved back to Minnesota. All the kids had settled there. When we arrived, we changed churches.

The Woodbury church had been our home congregation from the time of our first arrival in Minnesota in 1987 until we went back to Florida. I served as one of two elders there for much of that time and the church had grown to be the largest of our group in Minnesota – maybe 250 people.

That is where I took some joy in the diversity of some of our gatherings. We had four different home languages. In addition to the Hmong children who came to our special events, Hispanic and deaf groups each met simultaneously with the English-speaking group.

When we came back to Minnesota, our oldest son, Michael, asked us to join with the little Eagan group where he worshipped. Eagan has about 30 people on a good Sunday morning. We have no building and don't want one. We meet in an elementary school the first two Sundays of every month and in a senior living facility the other Sundays. Alex, as he grew up, was a part of the Woodbury youth group and Charlene maintained her relationship with their women's group. She is teaching a weekly Bible class for them now.

I serve as the Eagan church's "Outreach Coordinator". That term means whatever I want it to mean from time to time, but basically it lets me try to point the activities of the church outside the building, away from our group toward the community at large. I attend the monthly area-wide preachers' meetings and am seen as something of a volunteer assistant to Tommy Carr, our minister.

Michael

Michael is the son who had just graduated from high school in 1986 before we moved to Minnesota in

January 1987. He stayed behind in Tallahassee. He tried an art school and the local community college, but neither appealed to him. He worked at a video rental store at a time when video stores were just coming into their own. When the owners moved away, leaving the store behind, Michael was left to manage it.

Michael was very connected to our church, which was located next door to Florida State University. Through the influence of the church staff he decided he wanted to be a campus minister. He went off to Searcy, Arkansas, to attend Harding University where he got a Bachelor's degree in Bible. By that time, he had gotten to know Diane Roof. Diane, also a student at Harding, was from a St. Paul suburb and the two shared many 12.5-hour trips in various carpools. She is now his wife and they have a son, David, 16.

Michael decided at some point that he didn't want to serve at the mercy of a local church, a feeling I share. He is the Sunday morning Bible class teacher at Eagan; he coordinates our annual retreat; and he oversees the Sunday evening activities for the church while working in customer service for a local corporation.

Michael has also made a name for himself in the comic book world. He has just published a graphic novel, "Kill All Monsters!", available from Amazon.

Mark

I mentioned Mark and Matt in the introduction. Mark is a Saint Paul police officer. He has been married twice and neither situation has turned out well for him. He has two wonderful children both in the high school near where their mother lives. Kevin is a senior and is active in the Police Explorer group that is sponsored by his dad's department. He just joined the Wisconsin National Guard. Rachel is in special needs classes. She is delighted to be in the same school with her big brother. Everyone she sees is a friend and she is well loved by her community.

Matt and Alex

Matt has a bachelor's degree in psychology and has worked on a Masters in Marriage and Family Therapy. He is a Personal Care Attendant for people with disabilities and is also building his own business giving drum lessons in a local music store. Many of his drumming students are special needs kids. He is good at it and the kids love him. Matt has a delightful wife, Brandy, and a stepson, Josiah.

Alex

Alex, Matt's son, is married to Abigail. He has finished his degree and she is working on hers. He lived with me and Charlene for several years.

Matt had Alex when he was 20 and was about to go off to college. Alex was about to be adopted when Matt was told he would soon be a father. Matt finally came to us and told us, "I have a son." He desperately wanted to raise Alex, but knew he didn't have the resources. We told Matt we would be his backup if he wanted to raise him. He did and we were.

When Alex's mother, Kathy, told Matt he was going to be a father, she had already made an agreement with a local adoption agency, knowing that she did not have the resources to raise a child on her own.

Matt did not tell us until after Alex was born. Thinking he had no right to interfere, he conceded to the adoption plan. But as time grew closer to finalize the adoption, he found he couldn't agree. As it turned out, the county had ignored Matt, assuming that a father would have no interest. Kathy had already picked out a potential adoptive family.

I called the adoption agency to tell them that Matt wanted to raise his son, but they were not responsive.

I figured out pretty quickly that they did not want to disrupt the placement they had made.

I was the Social Services Director for Ramsey County and Alex's mom lived in neighboring Washington County. I called my counterpart there and asked him for a reference to an attorney who was an expert in family law and who was well respected by the juvenile court there.

My counterpart gave me two options. One attorney was a good negotiator who was great at reaching agreements between parties. The other was a fighter. The situation was not something that could be negotiated. One side had to win and the other side would lose. I chose the fighter.

The court process was scary, but the outcome was in our favor. The judge read his order in open court. He said that Alex would be transferred to Matt's custody by 2:00 P.M. on a given date. It wasn't until we were walking out of the courtroom that Charlene checked the calendar and discovered that the given date was that very day.

Charlene

I have mentioned Charlene throughout the book. She is an amazing woman whom God put in my life. We have been married for 52 years.

Charlene loves God above all else, me included. Then she loves people – all kinds of people. She will befriend anyone. She has mentored untold numbers of people throughout our marriage, Black, White and Asian - particularly young women. Lots of people call her "Mom," including a number of Haitian young men and women. And she is a great cook and baker, a skill she uses constantly to help others. Her love for people has brought her a lot of grief on their behalf, but she plows on, loving particularly those who need it most because no one else loves them.

Mick's and Ricky's stories are told in Chapters 18 and 17, respectively.

Chapter 20

A Piggyback Ride; Nigeria and Cameroon

Richard Inyang and I became friends because of our common love for Jesus and his church. Richard is the preacher for the Roseville Church of Christ here in Minnesota. He has had some difficulties since agreeing to be the local preacher there. The church had been predominately White and had split a few years before. The small group of people left there were greatly discouraged. I commiserated with him for several months.

I became really excited when he started telling me of his planned return to his home country of Nigeria and to Cameroon where he has done mission work for several years. He invited me to come along.

The last time a White person had been scheduled to go to his home congregation had been several years before and that trip was cancelled because of fear of Boko Harram, a military group trying to take over the country. The church there wanted a White visitor to break the ice so other White folk would feel better about visiting.

The plan was to visit with Richard's home congregation and then go visit many of the little congregations in Cameroon that he had helped establish. Richard told me that I would need a visa to get into Nigeria, but that one was not needed to enter Cameroon, if you were entering from Nigeria. It turned out that was true, if you were Nigerian.

We flew into Nigeria, made a few visits first, then went to Richard's home congregation. The church had a sign out front proclaiming that it was the first Church of Christ in Nigeria. As it turned out, there was a hospital close by, sponsored by an organization directed by Tom Carr, a friend of ours from Searcy, Arkansas. We visited the hospital and I determined to raise money to replace the mattresses throughout.

Our reception in Nigeria was very different from the one in Haiti. I didn't detect any of the mistrust we experienced in Haiti. Richard's parents killed a goat in our honor and had the whole church over for dinner. On Sunday morning, Richard and I were presented with elegant, traditional Nigerian garments. I taught the class and Richard preached. Richard's brother said after the service that he wanted to be baptized. Richard said he had been preaching to him for years. Several of us went down the road a bit to where the road crossed a stream and, next to some people bathing and others washing clothes, Richard baptized his brother. Then we went back to the building where the rest of the church was waiting and had the Lord's supper. It was a happy day.

Cameroon

Then, our business finished in Nigeria, we set out for Cameroon by boat. The open boat had a lot of baggage and cargo stacked right behind my head and more people than there was room for in front of me. It was 104 degrees and the ride was four hours long in the direct sun. I had no hat. My backpack, medications and water bottle were out of reach. It was my own fault, but by the time we got to the little port in Cameroon, I was dehydrated and was very sick. Since a surgery in 1994, I have had to balance all my hormones artificially and this trip had severely unbalanced them.

We went into the small customs building where there was one customs official. He asked me for my visa. As it turns out, a Nigerian citizen does not need a visa to get into Cameroon, but an American does. The official said we would have to return to Nigeria. I asked him to let us fly back, knowing that another boat ride could do me in, but his answer was that we had to return in the same way we had come over. By phone, I talked to a Marine in the U.S. Embassy in Cameroon, but he said the embassy has no influence over Cameroonian immigration.

The Life Saving Piggy Back Ride

I took extra salt and steroids and drank extra water, but by that time I was in bad enough shape that I needed an IV. We slept on the floor and took the boat back the next morning. When we finally got back to Nigeria, I was getting weaker and weaker. I suggested that Richard and I share a room that night, knowing that I might get to a point where I could not function.

I did get sick enough that I was about to pass out, with a coma not far behind. I have been admitted to hospitals in Port au Prince, Nigeria, Miami and Saint Paul for this condition.

Richard got in touch with a local hospital and found a physician willing to meet us there. We had to pull over a couple of times on the way to the hospital for me to throw up. When we got to the hospital, the emergency room was on the third floor and by then, I was not able to walk. Richard carried me piggyback to the third floor. He is a head shorter than I am.

The hospital staff found the saline solution and the hydro-cortisone I needed and started the IV. I don't remember much of the time I spent there, but Richard got our return tickets, talked with Charlene and we went to the airport. I had gotten enough medication to be able to make it home, cutting our trip short by about two weeks.

Richard saved my life. His oldest son, Jonathan, is in junior high school and his two twin boys are in pre-school. One of the twins is named David, after me. As Richard was carrying me up those stairs, he didn't see himself carrying a White man; he was carrying his brother.

Chapter 21

My Books

I have four books in print, all of them aimed at encouraging Christians to move out of the "go along to get along" mode and to hold up a light in the darkness. About the time I retired in 2006, something was eating at me. I saw church buildings everywhere, but around the world people were starving. There is enough food grown in the world to feed us all, but it is not reaching those with the greatest need.

Driving across southern Georgia one morning, we were seeing church building after church building, many of them with steeples and with signs saying "Come worship with us." It seemed very competitive and I knew that was not what Jesus had in mind. He had prayed that we would all be one (John 17:20-21). In my first book I particularly attacked the practice of building fancy buildings with steeples while people starve across the water or around the block and while people die of preventable diseases.

Churches are failing at their greatest mission. When Jesus described the judgment, he described it as a separation of "sheep" and "goats".

The sheep in his analogy are those of us who feed the hungry, get water to the thirsty, give sanctuary to the refugees and immigrants, tend to the sick and those in prison, get clothes to those who need them, and visit people who are sick or in prison. They go to an eternal kingdom prepared for them from the beginning (Matthew 25:31-36). But today many churches offer complex excuses for not reaching out. We need to forget our rationales and "Just Do It".

So, in 2007, I published a book titled *A Call to Arms! Out of the Pews and Into the Streets*. We were living in Palm Beach County at the time. Here is a quote:

> *"In the last year there have been 15 murders of young Black men in the north end of West Palm Beach. One woman was also killed in the same area and the same time period. All of them were shot. The victims ranged in age from 16 to 29. The average age was 21. The Black ministers have done their usual marches,*

> *summits, conferences, and calls for action. Local officials have done their usual 'Oh, my, how awful!' speeches with promises of tougher law enforcement. The White ministers throughout this county of 1.3 million people have been too busy to notice. We White Christians go about our business, thankful that it is not in our neighborhood."*

The question on the back cover reads: "Is the Church's inward focus robbing the poor?" It goes on to proclaim, "It is time for the church, with or without its current leaders, to challenge Satan in his strongholds by returning to its mission – helping the helpless, effecting rescues, and spreading good news."

Book two came along three years later, in 2010. It seems that the world was not changing very rapidly as a result of book one. The question was, "Who will lead the church that is entangled in its own organizations into the war against Satan?" Jesus had said that the very gates of Hell would not prevail against his church (Matthew 16:18), yet the church was hunkered down in its pews. Where are the bold leaders? The answer is that you are the bold leaders.

Entitled *Prostitutes, Tax Collectors and You,* my second book makes the point:

> *"Church leadership is not about committee meetings, goals, plans or dynamic speakers. It is instead about people of integrity seeing what needs to be changed in this world and setting out to change it. Jesus used prostitutes, tax collectors, fishermen, insurrectionists and reformed religious leaders to carry on his work when he finished his three-year demonstration project here and went home. We are now his people here and it is our job to lead this army in solving the problems he identified: hunger, thirst, sickness, imprisonment and immigration."*

The third book was born of my dissatisfaction with the image of Christianity being portrayed to America. We were being seen as frustrated, would-be, political reformers whose agenda was too far outside the mainstream to make any headway and who were totally defeated by the thought. The book is titled *Peace on Earth?* Note the question mark. The subtitle is "Relax Christian, God still has your back".

The premise of *Peace on Earth?* is that the peace Jesus promised us comes from within us, not from our circumstances. The cover image was drawn by our daughter-in-law, Diane. In it, our grandson, David is playing peacefully on the banks of Lake Superior with a storm brewing behind him.

The book goes on to make the perhaps controversial point that we are not called on to legislate our neighbors into morality. Rather by teaching we are to bring the masses into Jesus' loving arms (Mark 16:15 et.al.)

The fourth book is a quick read, 58 pages long. I have preached it as a sermon, covering most of the salient points. Entitled *Does the Church Really Have Good News?* it is designed with two purposes in mind: 1) to describe five promises God made for us that we can claim in this life and 2) to show that we don't have to start off our evangelistic effort with a description of Hell. And because it is so short, it will make a great handout to someone you know who is questioning. All four books are available at amazon.com/author/davidmay.

You have book number five in your hand.

Chapter 22

Reconciliation Reconsidered

That pretty well finishes the historical portion of my story. The rest is current. I have begun to be more verbal about what I see as the need for White Christians to stand up for Black people. I developed a sermon centered on Jesus' telling of the story about the Good Samaritan and have presented it to three local congregations so far. The gist of it appears in Chapter 23.

In the last months of 2016 I led a Sunday evening class for our little local church, reviewing Tanya Smith Brice's book *Reconciliation Reconsidered*. The book is a collection of 12 essays in three sections, looking at Historical Realities, Contemporary Challenges, and Concrete Examples. The sub-title is "Advancing the National Conversation on Race in Churches of Christ."

All my previous books, in one way or another, are aimed at and are about the church. I have been careful in each of them to be sure that they were more broadly applicable than to the Churches of Christ. But here was a book on a topic that I was interested in and that was very directly aimed at my faith tradition. It felt closer to home. It was not about "the church" in general, it was about us and it was not pretty. The essayists are professors and deans of Universities as well as authors and consultants. They paint a picture of White churches during the reconstruction who "helped" Black churches fund their church buildings and their preachers as a way of maintaining separation.

Minneapolis Central

At the end of the study we agreed that we wanted to get to know the members of the Minneapolis Central Church of Christ which is predominately Black. We decided to find out what activities Central was involved in and that to offer to help. Because *Reconciliation Reconsidered* had pointed out that most collaborative efforts between Black and White churches were planned and administered by White folk, we wanted to be careful not to follow that pattern.

So far seven of our thirty members have been involved. That may seem like a small number, but it is 23% - not a bad showing for a new start-up ministry. We have helped with a four-day Vacation Bible School, a one-day Bible Bowl, and with a breakfast for a local homeless shelter. All three of these efforts were planned and organized with no thought of help from White churches. Yet, we were able to be of some assistance and I believe our presence was appreciated. We are beginning to make friends with people from the Central church, which was one of the original goals.

It is a start, but a small start, and just a start. Through my whole life I have looked for the "big picture". When I worked for the State of Florida, I was looking for ways to help all the kids in the state. The whole time we were working in Haiti, I was looking for ways to help Haiti as a whole. Roberta, the woman who gave up everything to work there, said that she was sent there, not to fix Haiti, but rather to help whomever God put in front of her that day. I have tried to adapt that view, without totally losing the larger view.

Paper Bags for Panhandlers

Charlene and I have put together small brown paper bags to hand out to the panhandlers we see so often in downtown Minneapolis and Saint Paul. In each we put several kinds of food including meat, fruit, crackers, cookies, and a granola bar; a napkin; a spoon; a pair of socks; a tooth brush; toothpaste; two dollars and a 3X5 card with this quote from Jeremiah 29:11-14:

> *"This message is from the Lord. I have good plans for you. I don't plan to hurt you. I plan to give you hope and a good future. Then you will call my name. You will come to me and pray to me and I will listen to you. You will search for me, and when you search for me with all your heart, you will find me. I will let you find me."*

We don't put any contact information in the sack because we don't want to appear to be entering the competition for members or for attendance.

Black Lives Matter

We went to the Minnesota State Fair three times this year. On two of those trips I had opportunity to chat with someone in the Black Lives Matter booth. We agreed that good communication is the beginning of an answer and that facilitating communication is an important contribution someone can make. I wanted to get the contact information for the young man I was speaking with, but he was evasive. I assume that was for safety reasons.

Coffee with a Cop

About two weeks later, Charlene and I went to "Coffee with a Cop" in TK's Coffee right down the street from where we live. Turns out, the cop is the local Police Chief and we were the only people who showed up. We were with her for about an hour and a half, and she is sympathetic to the Black Lives Matter movement. I am thinking, if I can get back in touch with the BLM representative from the fair booth, we could have a good conversation.

The chief does that every month. We have rejoined her monthly since and will likely continue to do so. I am trying to come up with some way to insert myself into the local conversation about race relations, perhaps as the "Retired Social Services Director" for Ramsey County.

TCDC and the Book Club

The Woodbury church recently hosted a weekend Twin Cities Discipleship Conference (TCDC) that ended back at the Black Minneapolis Central on Sunday night. There, a panel discussed race relations and the church. As a member of the panel I mentioned the book *Reconciliation Reconsidered* that we had studied at Eagan. Another panel member, a woman from the Central church, suggested that we set up a book club and that we start with that book. Several signed on. The goal of the group is much broader than reviewing books.

Chapter 23

WWJD?

This chapter is the gist of that sermon I delivered to three local churches in the last few months.

It is a very outdated expression, but I still like to try to follow it. In the 1990s, young people began wearing bracelets with the letters "WWJD" on them, signifying the question: "What Would Jesus Do?" It was and is a valid question for those of us who want to do the right thing.

In this instance, since I was educated to be a teacher, I like to study Jesus' life, looking for teaching methods that he found effective in his day. Here is one that is particularly relevant to our discussion.

The topic is race relations and the church. I want to consider the subject by looking at how Jesus approached race relations in his teaching and how the early church dealt with it. It was a problem for them and it is still a problem for us.

The Good Samaritan

The text is Luke 10:25-37. The story is that of the Good Samaritan. But what often gets missed in that story is the apparent contradiction in the title. Of course, the title wasn't included in the original writing, but the title is an accurate description of what happens.

To the Jewish people of the day Samaritans were not good. They were to be avoided. They were not to be spoken to; you could not do business with them; and a respectable Jewish person would not even be seen having a conversation with one. The Jews took the long way around to avoid the area where the Samaritans lived. The Samaritans were a mixed race and were considered to be lower than the Gentiles.

According to their teaching, a Jew was under no obligation to help any Gentile who was in need and, in fact, if a Jew killed a Gentile, the guilty Jew could not be put to death. The laws are different today, but I encourage you to think in terms of Black people and White people as we consider this account.

When Jesus was confronted by a lawyer who set out to "test" Him, He told the story of the good Samaritan. The lawyer knew the answer to the question he asked Jesus, "What must I do to inherit eternal life?" And when Jesus turned the question back to him, he gave the correct answer: "'Love the Lord your God with all your heart, all your soul, all your strength, and all your mind.' Also, 'Love your neighbor the same as you love yourself.'"

The lawyer was trying to trick Jesus into saying something that would get Jesus in trouble with the religious leaders. But then, to keep from looking so foolish, he asked Jesus a follow-up, defensive question, "Who is my neighbor?" I can see him looking around at his audience as he asked it, "Who is my neighbor?"

Jesus answered with the story of the Good Samaritan. By all indication, the injured man was a Jew, yet the Priest and the Levite passed by on the other side of the road. These were people who should have been teaching compassion to their constituents. They were obligated to stop and help, yet they got as far away from the needy man as they could. It was the Samaritan who stopped to help the injured man.

Jesus could have reversed the roles in this story and still had a powerful illustration. The Samaritan could have been the injured party. In fact, that would have been the more direct way to illustrate the point about neighborliness. But Jesus didn't tell the story that way; he took the illustration a step further and made the Samaritan the good guy.

Why do you suppose Jesus made the story go this way? Why would he make the Samaritan out to be the hero, contrary to the way Samaritans were viewed by the Jews, and very probably by this lawyer to whom he was telling the story?

He was clearly trying to teach something to this lawyer and to the others who were listening. By choosing the man who was looked down on, both racially and religiously, to be the good guy, Jesus made an important point. The lawyer had just admitted that the way to eternal life included loving your neighbor as yourself. And in answer to the question, "Who is my neighbor?", Jesus made the neighborly person be from the group that was most looked down on. He made the one likely to inherit eternal life turn out to be from the social, religious, and ethnic class that the lawyer doubtless hated.

How could Jesus have made this point any clearer? Regardless of their ethnic, religious and cultural beginnings, everyone is precious to God. And anyone who legitimately needs help is worthy of our assistance. When we are the helper, that puts us in a "one up" position and we can feel good about ourselves. By making the Samaritan the helper, Jesus crossed that boundary and made him "one up" in a good way in a society where he had always been ignored, put down, profiled, passed over and discriminated against.

I want to illustrate this point with additional scriptures revealing the teachings of Jesus, God, and the New Testament writers as they argued for racial inclusiveness. But before I do that, let's look at where this leads us today.

Race Relations Today

Race relations seem to be going backwards today. There was a time not so very long ago when we could pretend that everything was getting better and that soon race would not be an issue in America. But today shootings of Black people by police officers seems to be higher than ever. That is surely in part because the media has their antenna up and every local incident now gets national attention. But beyond that, there seems to be a real increase.

Part of the increase might be attributed to an increased reluctance on the part of young Black people to follow the lead of their elders to just go along and do whatever the police officer tells them to do, regardless of the obviously discriminatory, racially-based motives of some officers.

Yes, there are some racist police officers; just as some of the Black people being shot were shot by well-meaning public servants who were merely defending themselves or others. And yes, in the rhetoric, the innocent officers get lumped in with the racist ones, while the bad actors get lumped in with the innocent victims. Those of us who over-reach in our generalizations contribute to the misunderstandings between the two groups.

Peter and Cornelius

Let's look at more ways the Bible deals with the issue. Take the story of Peter and Cornelius, the Roman Centurion (Acts 10:1-48). Now Peter had been travelling with Jesus for three years. He knew Jesus taught the Samaritan woman at the well – the woman he was not supposed to be talking to - in the place he was not supposed to be. And how he sometimes healed non-Jewish people.

But when it came down to responding to Cornelius' invitation, Peter had to have a vision from heaven and a voice from the Spirit to get him to go. The Spirit made it clear in this passage that the gospel was for everyone. What convinced Peter finally was the fact that Cornelius and his whole household received the Spirit just as the apostles had on the day of Pentecost. Peter used that fact to convince his brothers back in Jerusalem (Acts 11:1-18).

One Flock

Jesus, throughout his ministry, kept saying, "the gospel is for all," just like the song we sing. He kept hinting and outright stating that the Gentiles would be brought into his kingdom. In John 10:16 Jesus says, "I have other sheep, not of this flock." He goes on to say that in the future there will be one flock and one shepherd. Some like to think he is talking about aliens from space here, but it probably a reference to non-Jewish believers.

He said, "One flock and one shepherd," yet, even in the churches of Christ, we have a Black flock and one that is largely White with a handful of Black people. It has been said that Sunday morning at 10:00 is the most segregated hour of the week. And it goes further. Our Black brethren have their own Bible college, their own annual national gatherings and their own national youth conference. They are more comfortable there. Their culture is not our culture; our culture is not their culture. Even after living together as free people for 150 years, and after over 50 years of integrated schools, our cultures are still different enough that we are really not comfortable in each other's settings.

That is a hard one to break. Who is going to give first? Even our politics are different. Black church people tend to vote Democratic these days while White church people tend to vote Republican. Crossing the Democratic/Republican boundary may prove to be harder than crossing the barrier of who leads our services and how we sing our songs.

Side-By-Side Haitian Churches

But are we called on to give up? There were two churches, both churches of Christ, in Haiti that met side by side. I discovered this fact one afternoon when I showed up early and alone for a Wednesday night service. There was a middle school student there that I didn't know but who knew enough English to carry on a rudimentary conversation. We ended up walking around the grounds and met a young boy next door – just across the fence. In conversation with him I discovered that there was a small church meeting there.

I spoke with some of the leaders of the larger congregation and was told that they had talked to the little church, albeit years ago, and that the little church didn't want to talk about merger.

Charlene and I visited with the little church a few times, while the larger group was meeting next door. We had some meetings of representatives of both groups, but the little group was still afraid. They were mostly scared that they would lose their identity and would forfeit all control. I gave up. But by this time an Alabama missionary named Larry Waymire was aware of the situation and he persevered. Through Larry's leadership, there is now one church where there were two and the song leader from the little church leads most of the singing at the combined services. As it turned out, that was one of the major, unspoken, hang ups. The song leader wanted to be able to continue leading the singing.

"All Things to All People"

I told that story to illustrate that giving up on fellowship should not be one of the possible options in our catalog.

Jesus prayed in the garden that we would all be one, just as he and God are one. Do you think he was thinking about the difficulty the early church would have with Jewish churches and non-Jewish churches? Or what about Black churches and White churches in the 21st century? Would that be a part of it?

And when Paul wrote to the church in Corinth, he chastised them for the way they were treating each other. In 1 Corinthians 11:17, he said, "Your meetings do more harm than good." Ouch! That hurts. They were apparently having what we might call a potluck meal. Yet each person or family ate only what they brought. Some were bringing huge meals, some were becoming drunk and some were going away hungry.

Do you see what was going on here? There were different classes of people in the same church. And the lower-class people were left hungry, in spite of Jesus' instructions to the contrary.

We have used this passage to figure out which element of the Lord's Supper to pass around first and to be sure we do remember the Lord as we should. Have we also missed a larger instruction here, that the whole church is despised when we shame those who have less? I encourage you to pay attention to what is going on around you. Apparently, the Corinthians had not noticed the effects of what they were doing. Not noticing may be our greatest sin.

So, what are we to do? In 1 Corinthians 9:20-22, Paul said, "To the Jews I became like a Jew to win the Jews... To those not under the law I became as one not under the law so as to win those not having the law (the Gentiles)... To the weak I became as weak to win the weak... I have become all things to all people so that by all possible means I might save some."

Paul learned how to communicate cross-culturally. Can we not do the same? He learned how to be like the people he was with. Remember, our goal is not to eliminate the Black churches. They are at least as legitimate a response to God as what we say and do in our White churches on Sunday morning. But we do want them not to feel isolated. And for us not to feel isolated from their culture.

What Should the Church Do?

As the rhetoric escalates, what is the role of the church? First, let's review the definition of church. When some think of "the role of the church", they think of an organization, often headquartered far away somewhere. Or at least they think of the appointed leadership of the local church, who have their meetings and decide the direction and goals the church will pursue. In either case, the role of the church is something very much beyond our control. It will be decided by someone else, somewhere else. But we know from scripture that we are the church (e.g. 1 Corinthians 12:12-31). The church is all of us. We don't really have the luxury of passing the buck to someone else.

So, if we are the church, what is our role in race relations in the U.S. in the last half of the 2010's?

First of all, do no harm. We need to thoroughly examine our attitudes and our conversations. "God so loved the world that he gave his only begotten Son, that whoever believes in him shall not perish, but shall have eternal life" (John 3:16, NASB). And he called on us to love the world too, regardless of race. We should think about our attitudes, particularly as they are reflected by our actions.

Be alert to what is going on around you. Step in to bring peace, harmony and love to every situation, whether it is a brief encounter in Wal-Mart or a major incident of disrespect shown on a street corner, on public transportation or in your office.

When you walk into a room, notice who is standing or sitting with whom. Is there a small group of Black people in one corner and the rest of the room is full of White people? Or is there one Black person by himself, being ignored by the larger group? Go over and make yourself known.

And in conversation, when someone makes a racist comment, at least don't make the appearance of agreeing. Hopefully you will be able to gently suggest an alternative way of looking at the situation.

Show generosity and love to all people wherever you are and whoever is there.

When I worked for Ramsey County, I publicly suggested that racism was stronger and deeper in Minnesota than it was down south. In the next few days a few Black employees came up to me individually to acknowledge that what I said was true. It is subtler here and is sometimes covered in a disguise of being "polite", but it is in some ways more vicious, while down south it is more in your face.

Keep your antennas up and be ready to come to the defense of anyone, red, brown, yellow, black or white, who is being pushed aside, left out, or, even worse, harshly treated. Don't let that kind of situation pass without taking some kind of a stand in their defense.

If you are White, seek out a Black person and determine to get to know them. If you are Black, make a White friend. Familiarity with people of other cultures is the first major step to breaking down barriers. Without this familiarity, we will not come to understand the churches they attend.

It may seem that I have made a giant leap – from Black people being shot and killed to "get to know a Black or White person," but that is where it has to start. We have to come to know and love each other. How do you change the world? One conversation at a time. Maybe you and your new friend can then come up with future steps toward reconciliation of Black people and White people in this nation.

We love the Lord. And we love his people, but we are not equally comfortable with all of His people. And they are not equally comfortable with us. And that contributes to the distance between us. That is where we need to start.

Chapter 24

Next Steps

So now what? What's next? As I have gotten older, dating back at least to the amazing start of the Saint Paul Urban Ministry, I have tried to be still and listen for God's promptings. To do that, I have had to sit on my desire to change the world all at once.

When we left Florida for the second time to move back to Minnesota, we made a list of reasons to move and reasons to stay. There were several seemingly major obstacles, but as we started planning and time went on, they started falling away, one by one. God was removing obstacles. Yet, sometimes, God is very still.

I think I can see God's hand in the still-forming relationship with the Central Church. Maybe there is something in our newfound friendship with the local

Police Chief. And, certainly, there are possibilities in our new, cross-cultural "book club".

Thurman Tucker is a friend. He is a Black man who is an elder in a near-by, mostly White, church. He told me recently that the majority has the responsibility to take the first step. That is true whether it is a Black church welcoming White visitors or a White community reaching out to its Black residents. And, of course, the minority group has the responsibility to be open and receptive.

One phrase that has been in the forefront of my mind for several months now has been, "Hold up a light in the darkness." Almost every prayer I have formed during this time period has included either: "Teach us to hold up a light in the darkness," or "Give us the courage to hold up a light in the darkness."

There is a lot of talk in the Bible about light and darkness. Darkness can stand for ignorance and light for wisdom or knowledge – "enlightenment", if you will. Holding up a light in that context would be spreading a little information. Maybe my Samaritan sermon falls in that category.

Light can also stand for righteousness and darkness for evil. Holding up a light in that case would be doing what is right, even though others are not. That rules out terrorism and guerilla warfare as possible approaches, but it includes taking some positions that others see as radical. I am still looking for the right opportunity to wear my "Black Lives Matter" t-shirt that I bought at the fair. By not wearing it around those who would misunderstand, am I being caring about their feelings, or am I going along to get along? That's my constant dilemma, not just about the shirt but about when to open my mouth and when to keep it shut. When and how do I hold up a light?

Both those ideas, knowledge/enlightenment and righteousness/evil, are a little fuzzy on the details. Publishing this book represents to me the adding of some knowledge to the issue and that is my next big step. If the book proves helpful, perhaps we can use it to open doors and begin conversation with our neighbors.

Chapter 25

In Summary

How do you sum up a life? Maybe I should write this part as if it were an obituary. All the church people I have been around in the last several years know that my favorite church song is "I'll Fly Away". I especially like the phrase "When I die, Hallelujah, bye and bye. I'll fly away".

More recently I've been telling people that, if I am ever in hospice, I want a small group to come in and sing Johnny Cash's song "Angel Band". The chorus goes, "Oh, come, angel band. Come and around me stand. Oh, bear me away on your snow-white wings to my immortal home." It needs to be done like Tanya Tucker does it. And don't let them change the last line to "snowy wings" like a lot of the covers do.

I frequently say that the four most important words in the Bible were uttered by the angel at the tomb. Speaking to the women, he said “He is not here!”, signifying that Jesus got up and walked out of the grave on a Sunday morning, proving once and for all that there is nothing in this world that we need to be afraid of.

That sums me up, but what about the world I grew up in? There are a lot of evil people in the world and a lot more who are misguided. Jesus says we should treat them all alike – we should love them and, where possible, redirect those who are misguided. I am still searching for ways to gently redirect people I meet along the way – whether in a coffee shop or as I stand in line at the grocery store.

This may be a strange time to bring it up, but throughout its writing I have been asked who is the audience for this book. Here is my best answer. I am writing it for Black people so that, like James Meredith, they can know that some of us are closet allies. I didn’t think that was a very noble goal, but a Black friend said it was admirable.

I do not imagine any White supremacists will read it, so it is not aimed at them. However, if you are one, maybe this will encourage you to reconsider your position.

I am writing it for White sympathizers, hoping to "spur them on to love and good works", like it says in Hebrews 10:24, perhaps to bring some of you out of the closet.

It is written for me. It is my way of solidifying who I am and what I am about. Not so much in case I forget, but more as a push forward.

And it is written for you, whoever you are, so that you will understand what it has been like growing up with White privilege, while knowing that there are generations of people growing up in a parallel universe with no privilege.

Don't get me wrong, I have had an exciting life. Every morning starts a new adventure for Charlene and me. Some of those adventures have led us to Haiti, to Africa, to Italy, to Viet Nam, to Florida, into court rooms (some told about here, some not), to counselors, in front of legislative committees and county boards, into hospital rooms and funeral parlors and to places we don't even remember any more. We continue to eagerly await tomorrow's adventure.

The Author

David May lives with his wife, Charlene, in a condo in Lilydale, Minnesota, just across the Mississippi River from Saint Paul. He is a former Marine Captain with time in Viet Nam. He is the retired Social Service Director for Ramsey County (Saint Paul), Minnesota, and also retired from the State of Florida having served as the state's Child Welfare Administrator and as the District Administrator for the Department of Children and Families in West Palm Beach.

David and Charlene have five children. The number of their grandchildren varies depending on who you count. Not wanting to leave anyone out, I will not give a number.

He has been a lifelong church member and has served as an elder in churches in Florida and Minnesota. Since his retirement, he has written five books, including this one. The others can be found at: www.amazon.com/author/davidmay.

Acknowledgements

Wow! To whom do I owe a thank you for this book? First would have to be Charlene, my primary editor, consultant and family history expert. If there is any order to the book that makes sense, the credit goes to her.

Then there are my volunteer reviewers and editors: Mike, Mark, Matt, Mick, Cordell, Charlene again and Linda Lingo.

Cordell Fischer, Bill Tatum, Thurman Tucker and Dr. Russell Pointer contributed great insight and confidence in my ability to join in this vitally important conversation in this way.

And then there is the crew at CreateSpace with their know-how and friendly advice on the myriad details.

Thanks to all of you!

89749097R00099

Made in the USA
Middletown, DE
18 September 2018